Summer Notebook.

Copyright © 1999 by Carolyne Roehm.

HarperCollins books may be purchased for
educational, business, or sales promotional use.
For further information please write
Special Markets Department
HarperCollins Publishers, Inc.
10 East 53rd Street
New York, NY 10022

First Edition

Design by Dina Dell'Arciprete-Houser
Written with Melissa Davis

ISBN 0-06-019387-5

99 00 01 02 03 ❖/HK 10 9 8 7 6 5 4 3 2 1

CAROLYNE ROEHM

Summer
NOTEBOOK

Garden Hearth Traditions Home

PHOTOGRAPHY BY
SYLVIE BECQUET
CAROLYNE ROEHM

HarperCollins*Publishers*

welcome to the
NOTEBOOK

If your life is like mine, you are constantly struggling to juggle a whirlwind of events and chores. Sometimes it takes every ounce of strength (and organization!) to make it through the day. In order to alleviate the chaos in my life, I came up with the idea for the Notebooks, a seasonal series of hands-on workbooks that you can use in every room of your home, from the kitchen to the garden. I have designed each Notebook to encourage readers to record his or her own notes in conjunction with the guidelines that I supply. Many times, the most successful methods evolve from many people's ideas. Although I am furnishing you with what has worked best for me in the past, it is up to you to create your own lists and ideas. There is space for trial-and-error notes, as well as room for clippings, ideas and advice that you'll want to remember from season to season, year to year. In the end, I hope you will be able to return to the Notebook for ideas on everything from planning the vegetable garden to tricks for extending the life of your cut flowers, and, we hope, you will be able to accomplish these tasks in a stress-free manner. This brings me to one of the most valuable lessons I have learned in life, which is to prioritize when taking on any new endeavor. I hope this Notebook for summer helps you sort out and organize the many ideas in your head, giving you more time to relax and enjoy your life.

CONTENTS

PERENNIAL
BORDER

I first saw Weatherstone on a beautiful October day while the smell of wood smoke wafted through the air of a glorious blue sky. As I explored the grounds, I discovered hidden beneath a hemlock hedge the remnants of what had been a perennial garden. Even this late in the season, a few flowers persisted. I was seduced by the fine bones of a potentially stunning garden. Seventeen years later, I am embarking on Perennial Border Revision Number Three. This once promising border has most certainly been a late bloomer. • Contrary to the belief that a perennial garden is enduring and low-maintenance, I find that of all my gardens it is the most time-consuming In fact, the only thing truly perennial about my perennial border is that it is the perennial object of my derision. Why don't my beds look like those at Sissinghurst? Why do my wan delphiniums rot? Why do my anarchic plants hop around at will? Why do some plants disappear altogether while others flourish with such vigor they choke out their neighbors? And where are those flowing swaths of harmonious color as dictated by Gertrude Jekyll? • I vow that next year I will rip up and redesign the perennial border. Where I used to dig in three plants to form a drift, I'll put in nine. Each clogged, overgrown clump will be surgically divided for optimum health and happiness. To make sure that the towering 'Pacific Giants' aren't hit with heat prostration, I will appeal to the gods and ask for an end to global warming And I will behave myself all winter if the gods listen. Such exemplary behavior should leave me plenty of time to reacquaint myself with colored pencils and graph paper.

MAINTAINING THE PERENNIAL
BORDER IN SUMMER

We are going to assume that all the very best attention was lavished on your perennial border in the spring and previous fall. Now you don't have to spend the summer doing remedial chores to catch up. Right? If so, you are unlike any gardener I have ever met.

Never mind. Your plants will still benefit from the following:

• Although it may be too late to rototill in those composted leaves you saved, it isn't too late to add organic nutrients to the soil. Use whatever composted matter you have as a mulch cover, but don't get the compost too close to the crown of the plants or it will attract rot. A two-inch layer of compost will supply nutrients to the plants, keep the soil temperature constant, and help retain moisture.

• Stake early in the season, before tall plants get uppity and won't bend to your will.

• Remember to keep perennials deadheaded for continuous bloom. Early-summer-blooming perennials should be cut back. If you are lucky you will get another show in late summer.

• Keep your beds looking sharp by edging with a "real" spade (a thin shovel with straight sides) in midsummer. Form a small trench with each cut and throw the soil from the trench onto the bed. This will form a little moat that will keep the grass from creeping into the border.

• Since you have so little else to do, get out there and weed. They are coming fast and thick, so attend to the invaders every other day. We recommend a distinctly earthy Château Souverain 1994 from the Napa Valley as a suitable accompaniment.

Favorite Perennial Plant List

Alchemilla mollis
Artemisia 'Silver King'
Aster 'Alma Potschke'
Buddleia 'Nanho Purple'
Caryopteris 'Worcester Gold'
Cimicifuga 'Brunette'
Delphinium 'Black Knight'
Dianthus 'Inchmery'
Echinacea purpurea 'Magnus'
Geranium himalayense 'Johnson's Blue'
Heuchera 'Palace Purple'
Iris germanica 'Batik,' 'Sapphire Hills,' and
  'Superstition'
Iris sibirica
Nepeta 'Dropmore'
Papaver 'Mrs. Perry'
Phlox 'Prime Minister'
Sedum 'Autumn Joy'
Thalictrum 'Lavender Mist'
Thyme 'Latavin Lucy'
Verbascum 'Southern Charm'

personal notes:

My favorite color combination, green and purple, as expressed by Siberian iris and lady's mantle (*above*). The bottle green bench (*left*) is my usual perch where I watch the garden unfold each morning.

A few flowers of the bold salmon poppy 'Mrs. Perry' (*right*) stand out in the front of the border, proving you don't always need a drift of plants to make a statement. The tissue paper petals punctuate the bed, giving it focus. Normally, I would not couple salmon pink poppies with magenta loosestrife, but I like the startling impact. *Below:* another view of the border framed by the old hemlock hedge.

From top left: Iris sibirica (unnamed), Iris''Supreme Sultan,' *Iris sibirica* 'Snow Queen,' Iris 'Gold Alps,' Lupine 'Russell Hybrid,' *Nepeta* 'Dropmore Blue,' 'Queen Elizabeth' rose, peony 'White Cap,' *digitalis purpurea. Opposite:* Strong vertical elements should not be forgotten when designing a garden. The wooden tower brings geometrical order into the chaos of exuberent growth. The tower forces the eye upward and bisects the hemlock hedge backdrop.

I have tried many times to plant thyme in between the rocks of this path (*below*) but the soil is so compacted from decades of foot traffic that the herb never takes off. Next year I will dig up the whole path and start again.

I designed portable wooden gates (*above*) to keep the deer out of the perennial beds. However, the gates don't stop the dogs from burrowing pathways through the hemlock hedge into the perennial beds.

The perennial border has been plagued with challenges. Half of the enclosed space gets full sun, the other half partial shade. The grade changes midway, sloping eastward and causing drainage problems. The beds have also been a victim of greed. Every time I found a plant that took my fancy it was jammed in without thought of scale; I just kept cutting the beds wider and longer to accommodate the new plants. Before I had a cutting garden, I would rob the beds of delphinium, iris, and lupine to fill vases for the house. As if my interference hasn't been enough, the borders have been at the mercy of three different gardeners with widely divergent design motives. Then there is the dog problem and the deer problem.

I FEEL I AM ON AN ENDLESS QUEST FOR THE PERFECT PERENNIAL BORDER

My goal for the redesign of this blueprint of errors and experiments is twofold: to change the scale and to change the proportions. The perennial border is a confined but large space, so I have decided to ratchet up the size of the plantings and go for more height. Since it is time for many of the perennials to be divided, this will be an opportunity to paint longer swaths of color from isolated patches. Finally, I will conquer the dead space at the eastern end and fix the drainage problems crippling my beloved delphiniums.

personal notes:

Peony 'Festiva Maxima'

Peony 'White Cap'

Iris 'Rare Treat'

Lupine 'Russell Hybrid'

Iris sibirica 'Orville Fay'

Iris 'Proud Tradition'

Baptisia australis (false indigo)

Iris sibirica 'Caesar's Brother'

Scabiosa 'Butterfly Blue' (pincushion flower)

Lupine 'Russell Hybrid'

Aquilegia vulgaris (columbine)

Iris 'Sapphire Hills'

Polemonium (Jacob's ladder)

Geranium 'Johnson's Blue'

Lupine 'Russell Hybrid'

Nepeta 'Dropmore Blue' (catmint)

ROBBING THE PERENNIAL BORDER PAYS OFF

Although it grieves me to cut from the perennial border, I've snipped these beautiful lavender, white and pink flowers and placed them asymmetrically in the basket. It makes such a lovely grouping that I cannot resist bringing them into the house.

Below are listed some of my favorite perennials that you can draw from when making your border plans. Although I tend to stick to the traditional colors—blue, purple, pink, silver, white and soft yellow—some of you may want to use more striking colors, which I have also included.

RED

Astilbe 'Fanal'

Bee Balm (*Monarda*) 'Cambridge Scarlet'

Coralbells (*Heuchera sanguinea*) *Dianthus* 'Portrait,' 'Bat's Double Red'

Daylily (*Hemerocallis*) 'Red Reward,' 'Berlin Red,' 'Pardon Me'

Lobelia cardinalis

Lychnis 'Ruba Plena'

Oriental Poppy (*Papaver orientale*) 'Turkenlouis,' 'Beauty of Livermere'

Ornamental grass (*Imperata cylindrica*) 'Ruba'

Penstemon 'Firebird,' 'Flame'

Phlox 'Starfire'

Potentilla 'Gibson's Scarlet'

Valerian (*Centranthus ruber*)

Yarrow (*Achillea*) 'Paprika'

PINK

Astilbe 'Peach Blossom'

Baby's breath (*Gypsophila paniculata*) 'Flamingo'

Bee balm (*Monarda*) 'Croftway Pink'

Bleeding heart (*Dicentra spectabilis*)

Coneflower (*Echinacea purpurea*) 'Magnus'

Cranesbill (*Geranium*)

Daylily (*Hemerocallis*) 'Pink Lavender Appeal'

Iris 'Beverly Sills'

Mallow (*Malva*) 'Fastigiata'

Meadow rue (*Thalictrum aquilegifolium*)

Phlox 'Bright Eyes'

Pinks (*Dianthus*) 'Doris,' 'Bath's Pink'

Queen of the Prairie (*Filipendula rubra*)

BLUE-PURPLE

Balloon flower (*Platycodon*)

Bellflower (*Campanula persicifolia*)

Butterfly Bush (*Buddleia*) 'Black Knight'

Catmint (*Nepeta*) 'Six Hills Giant'

Centaurea montana

Delphinium Belladonna, Pacific Hybrid 'King Arthur'

Gentian

Geranium 'Johnson's Blue'

Globe thistle (*Echinops*) 'Taplow Blue'

Iris 'Blue Magic'

Iris sibirica 'Perry's Blue'

Monkshood (*Aconitum henryi*) 'Spark's Variety'

Russian sage (*Perovskia atriplicifolia*)

Salvia 'East Friesland,' 'Blue Hill'

Scabiosa 'Butterfly Blue'

Speedwell (*Veronica*) 'Sunny Border Blue'

YELLOW

Anthemis tinctoria 'Wargrave'

Coreopsis grandiflora 'Early Sunrise,' 'Sunray'

Coreopsis verticdillata 'Moonbeam'

Corydalis lutea

Daylily (*Hemerocallis*) 'Golden Chimes,' 'Stella d'Oro'

Delphinium semibarbatum

Euphorbia polychroma

Foxglove (*Digitalis lutea*), D. grandiflora

Goldenrod (*Solidago*)'Crown of Rays'

Iris 'Pale Primrose,' 'Gold Flake'

Lady's mantle (*Alchemilla mollis*)

Ligularia 'The Rocket,' 'Przewalskii'

Ornamental grass (*Carex elata 'Aurea'*)

Potentilla 'Golden Queen'

Rudbeckia 'Goldsturm'

Yarrow (*Achillea*) 'Coronation Gold'

SILVER

Artemisia 'Silver Mound,' 'Silver Queen,' 'Powys Castle'

Dianthus 'Pike's Pink'

Golden yarrow (*Eriophyllum lanatum*)

Lamb's ears (*Stachys*) 'Silver Carpet'

Lamium maculatum 'Beacon Silver'

Lavender 'Hidcote,' 'Munstead'

Ornamental Grass (*Helictotrichon sempervirens*)

GARDEN JOURNAL

DATE: --

GARDEN LOCATION: --

PLANTS: --

COMMENTS / RESULTS: ---

I am providing you with some garden grid paper to layout any beds and borders that you might be planning. I have not included my perennial border plant plan since it is in flux; I will be dividing and moving my plants this fall. When I make my new plan, there are several basic things I bear in mind:

- Site suitability; sun, shade, and soil requirements.
- Scale of plants; height and width and placement in the border.
- Number of plants needed to achieve desired effect.
- Blooming times of plants; will garden be interesting throughout the seasons?
- What is your color palette?
- Consider color, shape, and texture of the plant's leaves; how do they play off one another?
- Do you want to include nonplant elements such as a path, sculpture, or large pots as focal points?

ROSES

I have heard that a few gardeners scorn—or if that is too strong a word, ignore—roses. They say the blossoms are too hyperbolic and the plant too much in need of pampering. All I can say is too bad for them. To absorb the fragrance and form of the rose is to be enchanted forever. • My love for this flower is a passion that borders on obsessive addiction. My collection of roses has grown from an assortment of two dozen hybrid teas to more than 700 bushes, shrubs, climbers, and ramblers of more than a hundred varieties of old roses, English roses, hybrid perpetuals, floribundas, and grandifloras. They have taught me much over the last two decades. • I intensely identify with Georgia O'Keeffe when she says, "Still, in a way, nobody sees a flower, really. It is so small. We haven't the time. And to see takes time. Like to have a friend takes time." At this point in my life I am taking more time to see. Perhaps gardening does that to you. Whether you have a pot of basil on the back porch or a sea of roses, as a gardener you are just that bit further along in the process of learning to see. The more time I spend cultivating and tending my roses, the more I see that these flowers, in all of their beauty, bring me closer to the divinity of nature. Did I understate my obsession with roses? They are my religion.

Although we grow more than 100 varieties of roses at Weatherstone, I would never assume to be an expert in their care and feeding. Thousands of books have been written about the horticultural requirements of roses and their complicated classifications, and this is where I turn when I need a rosarian's expertise. It seems, however, that as soon as I learn the difference between a gallica and a damask, or a thrip and an aphid, the information slides out of my brain.

To appease the anxiety attack over my much-loved but high-maintenance roses, I decided I needed a Cliff Notes version of the rosarian's bible that tackled the who and the what (classification) and the when and the where (planting, care, pests, and diseases). Here are the lists I compiled to keep me on track.

PLANTING POINTS

- *Choose a site that gets at least 6 hours of sun and has good air circulation.*
- *Have the soil tested, especially for magnesium. If the soil is deficient in magnesium,*
  add 1 cup of Epsom salts to the soil around each plant.
- *Prepare the bed well, digging at least 2 feet down and amend with organic matter,*
  peat moss, and phosphorus for healthy root growth.
- *Soak bare-root roses for 24 hours in water with a little fish emulsion.*
- *After their bath, prune off dead canes and dead roots.*
- *Dig a hole deep enough to accompany the bush and about an inch of the bud union.*
  Hill up the soil at the bottom of the hole and spread out the roots atop the mound.
- *Fill the hole with amended soil while holding the rose in place. Be sure to cover the bud union with about an inch of soil.*
  Firmly press down soil to prevent air pockets.
- *Water thoroughly.*
- *If planting container-grown roses, follow the same instructions except remove the bush from the container,*
  even if the container is cardboard or peat, and do not prune roots or stems.

CARE

- *Keep bushes well watered and free of weeds.*
- *Deadhead frequently.*
- *Prune bushes in spring (when new leaves are about one inch long) with well-sharpened shears.*
  Remove dead and crowded canes.
- *Feed roses once a month with a balanced rose fertilizer. Stop feeding roses by the end of July.*
- *Hill soil around the base of the bush to protect it from winter chill.*

PESTS AND DISEASES

- *Apply fungicide every week to 10 days during the growing season (at first leaf break).*
  Call the Cooperative Extension Service for a spray recommended for your growing zone.
- *Rotate fungicide brands to prevent resistant strains of disease.*
- *Rake all diseased leaves off the ground and destroy. Do not compost diseased leaves.*
- *Spray aphids with insecticidal soap, nothing stronger or you will harm their predators, the ladybug.*
- *Hand-pick Japanese beetles or, if this is impossible, spray with Sevin.*
- *Do not spray fungicides or pesticides on sunny or windy days. Spray early in the morning.*
- *Try to select roses that are mildew- and blackspot-resistant.*

personal notes:

ROSE CLASSIFICATION CHART

CLASSIFICATION	CHARACTERISTICS	VARIETIES	SCENT
Albas (OF*) A	Upright, tall, vigorous, few spines, mostly double blooms, white or off-white. Hardy.	'Félicité Parmentier' 'Madame Plantier' 'Maiden's Blush'	Strong to light fragrance
Bourbons (OF) B	Repeat bloomer, large flowers, arching canes.	'Madame Isaac Pereire' 'Madame Pierre Oger' 'Boule de Neige'	Strong fragrance
Centifolias (OF) CF	"Cabbage Rose," taller than gallicas, drooping heads and leaves; mostly pink blossoms.	'Fantin-Latour' 'Tour de Malakoff'	Strong fragrance
Chinas (OF) CH	Ancestor of all modern repeat bloomers. Small blossoms change from light to dark, sparse foliage.	'Irene Watts' 'Madame Laurette Messimy' 'Mutabilis'	Light fragrance
Climbing C	Tall canes need support. Ramblers' canes more pliant. Some are everblooming.	'Dortmund' 'Iceberg' 'Golden Showers' 'New Dawn'	Mild fragrance
Damask (OF) D	Semidouble and double blooms. Larger, taller than gallicas.	'La Ville de Bruxelles' 'Madame Hardy' 'Marie Louise' 'Rose de Resent'	Powerfully fragrant
Floribundas FB	"Clustered flowered" large shrubs, everblooming. Very hardy.	'Angel Face' 'Betty Prior' 'Gene Boerner' 'Iceberg'	Light to intense fragrance
Gallicas (OF) G	Oldest cultivated roses; low shrubs prone to suckers. Blooms single or clusters, strong colors.	'Camaieux' 'Charles de Mills' 'Empress Josephine' 'Tuscany Superb'	Fragrant
Grandifloras GF	Tall stems, heavily clustered flowers larger than floribundas.	'Gold Medal' 'Pink Parfait' 'Queen Elizabeth' 'Tournament of Roses'	Light to medium fragrance
Hybrid Musks (OF) HM	Often a climber. Shrub for poor soil and shade. Produces hips.	'Ballerina' 'Buff Beauty' 'Lavender Lassie'	Musky fragrance
Hybrid Perpetuals (OF) HP	Marginally hardy, sprawling-to-upright habit, many-petaled flowers on short stems. Repeat flowering. Blackspot-susceptible.	'Baroness Rothschild' 'Baronne Prévost' 'Ferdinand Pichard' 'Paul Neyron' 'Reine des Violettes'	Fragrant

ROSE CLASSIFICATION CHART

CLASSIFICATION	CHARACTERISTICS	VARIETIES	SCENT
Hybrid Teas HT	Large blossoms, long stems, modern rose.	'Blue Moon' 'Mister Lincoln' 'Peace' 'Tiffany'	Some are fragrant
Miniatures MT	Ten to 18 inches, very hardy.	'Magic Carrousel' 'Minnie Pearl' 'Popcorn' 'Starina'	Little to none
Moss Roses (OF) MR	Centifolia or damask mutation, drooping foliage and flowers. Sepals have moss-like growth with pine scent.	'Gloire des Mousseux' 'Henri Martin' 'Mousseline' 'Old Pink Moss'	Strong fragrance
Noisettes (OF) N	Climbers crossed for larger flowers. Not hardy.	'Céline Forestier' 'Champney's Pink Cluster' 'Gloire de Dijon' 'Madame Alfred Carrière'	Good fragrance
Polyanthas PA	Low-growing shrubs to about 2 feet with clustered, small flowers. Very hardy, everblooming.	'Cécile Brünner' 'China Doll' 'Marie Pavié' 'Perle d'Or'	Little fragrance
Portlands (OF) PL	Nineteenth-century repeat bloomer. Compact shrubs, 3 to 4 feet.	'Comte de Chambord' 'Jacques Cartier' 'Portland Rose' 'Rose de Roi'	Very fragrant
Rugosa Hybrids R	Rugosa cross. Disease-resistant, very hardy, low-maintenance. Violet-rose flowers.	'Blanc Double de Coubert' Canadian Explorer Series 'Sarah Van Fleet' 'Sir Thomas Lipton'	Lightly fragrant
Shrub S	Vigorous, spreading bushes with recurrent single and double flowers. Low-maintenance.	'Alchemist' 'Bonica' 'The Fairy' 'Golden Wings'	Little to none
Species (OF) SP	Wild roses. Single blooms, low-maintenance, hardy, disease-resistant.	*R. eglanteria* '*Rosa Mundi*' *R. rugosa* *R. spinossissima*	Very fragrant
Teas (OF) T	Small leaves and stems. Not hardy. Suitable for frost-free climates.	'Anna Oliver' 'Catherine Mermet' 'Duchesse de Brabant' 'Lady Hillingdon'	Very fragrant
David Austin English Roses ER	Hardy, sturdy bushes; repeat blooming, old-fashioned blossoms.	'Mary Rose' 'The Pilgrim' 'Heritage' 'L. D. Braithwaite'	Very fragrant

*(OF) = Old-Fashioned

old roses

For the New England gardener, the hardiness of old roses is a blessing. Not only can they stand up to severe winter chill, they are also less prone to disease, therefore requiring much less work than modern roses. The downside is that they bloom only once—although there are some exceptions—but while in bloom they are blanketed with hundreds of fragrant blossoms (such as 'Madame Hardy,' above) that seem to hold on the bush for a good month to six weeks.

I tend not to use old roses in bouquets since the stems are rather short and the heads do not pose as well as the moderns. If I do cut them, they are primarily used in smaller bouquets where the small cluster of flowers exudes an outsized fragrance.

Larger old roses become so laden with flowers that their beautiful faces plunge to the ground—a sight that unnerves me. To avoid this, we build support frames of bamboo (*below*) around the shrubs to keep the heavy branches out of the soil. *Below left:* The old variety 'Rosa Mundi' is magic to me. I love to include varigated roses in a bouquet. They add tremendous geometric interest.

Favorite Old Roses

'Rosa Mundi' (S)
'Madame Hardy' (D)
'Fantin-Latour' (C)
'La Ville de Bruxelles' (D)
'Rose de Rescht' (D)
'Tuscany Superb' (G)
'Camaieux' (G)

Opposite page: The south side of the house with a view from the breakfast room is a perfect spot for a garden since it is warm, sunny and protected. This relatively small garden contains variegated *Hosta fortunei* 'Aureo-marginata' (which does surprisingly well in almost constant sunlight), white lilac, roses 'Winchester Cathedral,' 'Sally Holmes,' and 'Iceberg,' and white anemones.

As you can see, one gets surprises at times when a plant marked "white" turns out to be another color, as in the case of this pink foxglove that slipped into the white garden. I left it because I rather like that element of imperfection.

Right: In the larger white garden at the pool, the four corners are framed by trellis towers. 'Seagull' and 'Sea Foam' are starting their slow (due to our cold winters) climb up these frames. The white roses in this garden in addition to the climbers are 'Iceberg' and 'Blanc Double de Coubert.' 'Blanc' is a good landscape rose, and while I have cut it for vases, I find it less durable than 'Iceberg.'

Favorite White Roses

'Iceberg' (FB), *above center*
'Boule de Neige' (B)
'Sally Holmes' (S), *above right*
'Winchester Cathedral' (S, DA)
'Fair Bianca' (S, DA)
'Kiftsgate' (C)
'Seagull' (C)
'Sea Foam' (S)

Wish List for Next Year

'Sombreuil' (C)
'Hebe's Lip' (S)

white roses

Four years ago, I succumbed to the vogue of white gardens. Being a colorphile at heart, I had avoided the trend; ghettos of white flowers—even white roses—were of little interest to me. Then, during a visit to the Chelsea Flower Show, I found some beautifully sculpted sage green garden benches that spoke to me. Loudly. I responded: "Ah, this is the inspiration I need to finally do a white garden." They came home to Weatherstone and became the focal point of the white garden.

underplantings

Roses like companions, unless they are particularly greedy ones that grab up moisture and nutrients. They seem to sense that these lesser mortals at their feet enhance rather than detract from their singular beauty. In the front rose garden at Weatherstone we use the dainty chartreuse blossoms of *Alchemilla mollis* (lady's mantle) to intensify the pastel pinks of the roses. Purple Johnny-jump-ups, pansies, and *Nepeta* 'Dropmore' (catmint) not only contrast well with the bright pink roses, they also hide the thorny legs of the bushes. Companion plants also help cut down on the hazardous task of weeding underneath the prickly canes and are a good alternative to naked mulch chips.

Favorite Underplantings:

Catmint (Nepeta)
Coralbells (Heuchera)
Pinks (Dianthus)
Geranium
Johnny-jump-ups (Viola tricolor)
Lady's mantle (Alchemilla mollis)
Lamb's ears (Stachys byzantia)
Lavender
Miniature roses
Salvia
Thyme

The formality of the rose garden is tempered by underplanting that appears to be almost out of control. The more the lady's mantle spreads onto the thick pathways and the Nepeta flops, the better I like it . . . up to a point. I chose clipped boxwood borders to restrain the friendly chaos.

personal notes: ....

....

....

....

....

UNDERPLANTINGS RUN AMOK BRING
CHARMING CHAOS TO ORDER

yellow roses

Yellow was not a color often found in the realm of old roses, but with the advent of David Austin hybrids, I found the big, blowsy yellows cheerfully represented. Two of the best (opposite page), 'Graham Thomas' and 'The Pilgrim,' show well with bronze pansies, unripe raspberries and blueberries, immature apples, and viburnum berries. Pansy stems are not as long or as sturdy as rose stems and must be given support. I cluster three pansies into a five-inch plastic floral vial and push the vial pick into the floral foam. The raspberry stems get the same treatment.

Other Favorite Yellow Roses   *'Yellow Charles Austin' (DA), 'Golden Showers' (C), 'English Garden' (DA), 'Gold Medal' (GF)*

SEVENTEENTH-CENTURY DUTCH MASTERS HAVE BEEN MY MUSE FOR COMBINING ROSES AND FRUIT

A few cautions: Pansies are heavy drinkers, so the vials must be checked daily for refills. In addition, certain fruits, such as apples, give off ethylene gas that can shorten the life span of flowers.

Annie, ace gardener, keeps watch over 'Constance Spry' nearby the Weatherstone studio.

Favorite Repeat-Blooming Climbers

'Dortmund'
'Blaze'
'New Dawn'
'Cressida'

constance spry

My relationship with 'Constance Spry' (above and left), began on a trip to Mottisfont Abbey in Hampshire. It was love at first glorious sight and heady smell. The attraction remains strong, despite the fact that I am treated to its bloom only once a year. 'Constance Spry' was David Austin's first English rose introduction, a cross between a floribunda and a gallica. Although the pink peony blossoms set the standard for old-fashioned beauty, its failure to repeat blooming kept it from becoming a horticultural success. If Constance is reluctant to make an encore, she displays no such shyness as a shrub. The canes on the pergola outside my studio easily reach 14 feet and are smothered in fragrant flowers in mid-June.

The soft celadon greens of variegated ivy
and immature blueberries make a perfect foil
for the luscious pink of 'Constance Spry.'

PEACHES AND PEACH ROSES

An assortment of roses, including 'Distant Drums' (coral-pink), 'Tamora' (apricot-pink), 'Color Magic (pink) and 'Taboo' (red), play with the colors of a bowl of luscious peaches and yellow cherries. Each vase contains a handful of roses but their impact is enhanced by mating the similar colors of the fresh fruit and coordinating the pair of vases with the fruit bowl.

personal notes:

WHITE ON WHITE

While I adore color, I occasionally like to work with the simple combination of white and green. The pristine beauty of white clematis 'Marie Boisselot' and the damask rose 'Madame Hardy' is refreshingly clean and lovely.

personal notes:

RUSTIC VS FORMAL

A weathered wooden trough holds 'Double Delight' (bicolor white and red), 'Tradescant' (red, foreground), 'L. D. Braithwaite' (red), 'The Fairy' (pink spray), 'Lilian Austin' (coral), 'Graham Thomas' (deep yellow), 'Queen Elizabeth' (medium pink) and 'Grüss an Aachen' (pale pink). The humble rustic container works in well-balanced opposition to the opulent roses.

personal notes:

ROSES AND COMPANIONS

This bouquet is created with the favorite companion plants in front of my rose garden. (*Nepata*) 'Dropmore Blue,' assorted pansies, and *Clematis* 'Niobe' (wine) weave their way through 'Ferdinand Picchard' (variegated), 'Ballerina' (single pink), 'L. D. Braithwaite' (red), 'Tuscany' (crimson gallica), 'Louise Odier' (warm pink Bourbon) roses, and immature blueberries. The pansies are put into plastic vials (because their stems are too short), which I strategically place throughout the bouquet.

personal notes:

RANDOM AND RAMBLING

I mixed these roses as if I were walking through the garden, randomly selecting the flowers, and without consciously arranging them. The bouquet combines small sprays of rambling white 'Sea Foam' and a selection of my favorite English roses, 'L. D. Braithwaite' (red), 'Tamora' (apricot-pink), 'Lilian Austin' (coral), 'Mary Rose' (medium pink) and a single yellow 'Graham Thomas.' The vase is a blue-and-white export china jar.

personal notes:

BASKET WITH BLUEBERRIES

A wicker basket of softly colored yellow, coral, and peach roses is grounded with sprigs of blueberries. The roses are 'Heritage' (shell pink), 'Lilian Austin' (coral), 'English Garden' (yellow), and 'Sally Holmes' (single yellow).

personal notes:

BEDSIDE BOUQUET

A small cluster of garden roses and *Nepeta* 'Six Hills Giant,' a favorite companion plant in the rose garden, make a charming bedside bouquet. The roses are 'Graham Thomas' (deep yellow), 'The Pilgrim' (soft yellow), 'Raubritter' (pink), and 'Lilian Austin' (coral).

personal notes: _____

_____

_____

_____

_____

_____

COLOR MAGIC

'Color Magic' blossoms change from a blend of pink to deep rose to beige as they unfurl. Nine fully opened 'Color Magic' roses have started to fade, yet they still hold their beautiful hue in a French blue vase with a scrap of ribbon tied around them.

personal notes: _____

_____

_____

_____

_____

_____

One of the challenges of plotting a rose garden is deciphering the various hues of the pinks, reds, yellows, and apricots. The pictures in the rose books and catalogues can be deceiving. I have tried to clarify this for myself by making a chart of the various hues. Of course, color is subjective and climate can have an impact on color. For instance, David Austin notes that in warmer climates, a rose may be a true pink but that same rose in cooler climates may have more blue in it. My list is given only as a guideline.

CORAL PINK (warm pink with orange tones)
'Abraham Darby' (ER)
'Aloha' (C)
'Barbara Rose' (C)
'Belle Story' (ER)
'Bonica' (S)
'Comte de Chambord' (P)
'Lilian Austin' (ER)
'Newport Fairy' (C)
Rosa eglanteria (S)
'Sexy Rexy' (F)

BLUE PINK (cool pink with lilac tints)
'Pristine' (HT)
'Queen Elizabeth' (GF)
'Reine des Violettes' (HP)
'Tour de Malakoff' (C)
'Reine Victoria' (B)

MEDIUM PINK (true pink, neither warm nor cool)
'Baronne Prévost' (HP)
'Bow Bells' (ER)
'Charles Rennie Mackintosh' (ER)
'Color Magic' (HT)
'Constance Spry' (ER)
'Duet' (HT)
'First Prize' (HT)
'Gertrude Jekyll' (ER)
'Jacques Cartier' (P)
'Mary Rose' (ER)
'Potter & Moore' (ER)
'Queen Elizabeth' (GF)
'Raubritter' (GC)

SOFT PINK (shell pink to blush pink)
'Baroness Rothschild' (HP)
'Chaucer' (ER)
'Félicité Parmentier' (A)
'Grüss an Aachen' (F)

'Heritage' (ER)
'Kathryn Morley' (ER)
'Madame Louis Lévêque' (M)
'Fantin-Latour' (C)
'Madame Lauriol de Barny' (B)
'Madame Pierre Oger' (B)
'New Dawn' (C)
'Salet' (M)
'Souvenir de Malmaison' (B)

BRIGHT PINK
'Bonica' (S)
'Louise Odier' (B)
'William Baffin' (S)

YELLOW
'Bredon' (ER)
'Gloire de Dijon' (C)
'Gold Medal' (GF)
'Golden Showers' (C)
'Graham Thomas' (ER)
'The Pilgrim' (ER)
'Yellow Charles Austin' (ER)

APRICOTS AND CORALS
'Buff Beauty' (HM)
'Alchemist' (HM)
'Canterbury' (ER)
'Charles Austin' (ER)
'English Garden' (ER)
'Frontier Twirl' (HT)
'Music Mountain' (HT)
'Peace' (HT)
'Playboy' (F)

WHITE
'Boule de Neige' (B)
'Fair Bianca' (ER)
'Frau Karl Druschki' (HP)
'Iceberg' (FB)

'Kiftsgate' (C)
'Madame Hardy' (D)
'Rambling Rector' (R)
'Sally Holmes' (S)
'Sea Foam' (S)
'Seagull' (C)
'Winchester Cathedral' (ER)

RED
'Charles de Mills' (G)
'Dortmund' (C): red with orange
'Europeana' (F): red with orange
'Fisherman's Friend' (ER)
'L. D. Braithwaite' (ER): true crimson
'Mr. Lincoln' (HT): true crimson
'Othello' (ER): blue red
'Red Blaze'
'Rose de Rescht' (D): red to fuschia
'Rose du Roi' (P)
'The Prince' (ER): deep red
'The Squire' (ER): deep crimson
'Tuscany' (G): deep red, almost burgundy
'William Shakespeare' (ER): blue red

STRIPED
'Camaieux' (G)
'Rosa Mundi' (G)
'Variegata di Bologna' (B)

RED & YELLOW
'Double Delight'
Roses 'Constance Spry'

FAVORITE REPEAT-
BLOOMING CLIMBERS
'Dortmund,' bright red single
'Blaze,' red
'New Dawn,' soft pink
'Cressida,' blush pink

GARDEN JOURNAL

DATE: ---

GARDEN LOCATION: --

PLANTS: ---

COMMENTS / RESULTS: ---

FOURTH OF JULY

I miss the days when—with great excitement—my parents would take me to the local roadside fireworks stand and we would load up on sparklers, ladyfinger firecrackers, and Roman candles. My tougher cousins were always attracted to the heavy noisemakers like M-80s and cherry bombs. I was content with benign sparklers, flitting about with my lighted fairy wand while the cousins plotted their own big bang theories. In this age of caution, few firework stands are still open (although like everything else these days, fireworks are available through the Internet) to private consumers. We must content ourselves with less seditious Fourth of July activities: gathering with friends and family to devour lots of delicious American picnic food. If the gathering calls for potluck, I make sure to assign courses ahead of time to avoid the calamity of five potato salads and no dessert. Once the guest list is firm and the food is assigned, my job is to set the scene. Preparing the red, white, and blue background to a summer feast never bores me. Those basic three colors offer a world of design ideas and the iconic American flag is a stunning backdrop. While the assigned menu varies from year to year, I always include some form of fresh fruit pie or tart and homemade ice cream.

t The red, white, and blue of the Stars and Stripes is one of the most enduring American symbols. Betsy Ross deserves credit for having conceived of a color scheme and design that has remained modern. Even today, clothing designers have done well by appropriating her flag for their logos. Working within that tradition, I found navy and white and red and white plaid Irish blankets to use as tablecloths. Inexpensive tin splatterware plates proved valuable for their unbreakable durability. The striped white crock filled with a mix of simple red and white carnations stood up to the summer heat.

Menu: Pork kabobs with vegetables, black bean bake, green salad, blueberry-orange tart with fresh whipped cream, watermelon

PORK KABOBS
(Makes 10 12-inch Skewers)

    3 cloves garlic, coarsely chopped
    2 teaspoons ground cumin
    2 teaspoons ground coriander
    1 jalapeño pepper, finely chopped
    2 teaspoons salt
    ¼ cup olive oil, plus additional for grilling
2 to 2½ pounds pork loin
   20 whole small shallots
    2 Portabello mushrooms, stems removed, cut into
       1-inch cudes
    2 medium zucchini, cut into ½-inch rounds
    2 red, yellow, orange and/or green bell peppers,
       cut into 1½-inch chunks
   20 bay leaves (optional)

1. Place garlic, cumin, coriander and jalapeño, and salt in bowl of food processor. Pulse several times to chop and blend. Slowly add ¼ cup olive oil through the feed tube and process until a paste. Place mixture in a resealable plastic bag. Slice pork into 1-inch cubes and add spice mixture, thoroughly coating meat. Allow to marinate in the refrigerator for at least 1 hour, preferably overnight.

2. Thread 10 12-inch skewers alternating meat and vegetables (and optional bay leaves). Grill on medium coals for 15 to 20 minutes, turning occasionally, and brushing with a small quantity of olive oil.

Opposite: Neatly placed rows of blueberries top a very thematic Fourth of July tart. Yes, I did carefully place each berry stem side up, but at least I resisted the overkill of duplicating the flag. It's been done.

169 BLUEBERRIES LINE UP TO SALUTE THE AMERICAN FLAG

BLACK BEAN BAKE
(10 to 12 Servings)

    1 teaspoon plus 3 tablespoons olive oil
    1 tablespoon whole cumin seed
    ½ teaspoon ground cardamom
    1 large onion, chopped
    2 cloves garlic, minced
    2 red bell peppers, chopped
    1 fresh jalapeño pepper, seeded and finely chopped
    3 cups fresh corn kernels
    1 pound dried black beans, cooked and drained
One 28-ounce can whole peeled tomatoes, slightly
    crushed or 5 to 6 fresh tomatoes, chopped
    Juice and finely grated zest of 1 orange
    Salt and freshly ground pepper to taste
    ½ cup fresh chopped parsley
    ¼ cup fresh chopped cilantro

1. Preheat oven to 375°. Lightly grease 9-by-13-inch ovenproof dish with 1 teaspoon olive oil.

2. In a large skillet over medium heat, toast cumin seed for about 3 minutes or until very fragrant, stirring constantly to avoid burning. Add cardamom and continue stirring for 1 minute. Remove spices from pan and reserve.

3. In the same skillet over medium heat, add 3 tablespoons olive oil, add onions and garlic and sauté until onions are softened and slightly golden, about 7 minutes. Add red and jalapeño peppers and corn and sauté for 10 more minutes.

4. In a large bowl, combine sautéed vegetables and toasted spices with remaining ingredients and blend well. Place in prepared pan, cover and bake for 50 minutes. Uncover and bake for 10 additional minutes or until edges are bubbling. Serve hot.

BLUEBERRY-ORANGE TART
(6 to 8 Servings)

    1¼ cups all-purpose flour
    1 stick unsalted butter, melted and cooled
    4½ tablespoons powdered sugar
    5½ cups fresh blueberries
    1 cup granulated sugar
    Juice of and finely grated zest of 1 orange
    2 tablespoons quick-cooking tapioca

1. Preheat oven to 350°. In a medium bowl, combine the flour, butter and 3½ tablespoons powdered sugar. Press dough in a thin layer on the bottom and sides of an 8-inch square pan. Refrigerate for 30 minutes or until firm. Prick dough all over with a fork and bake crust for about 25 minutes, or until lightly golden. Remove from oven and cool.

2. In a medium-sized saucepan, combine 4 cups of blueberries, granulated sugar, orange juice and tapioca. Blend well and let stand for 15 minutes.

3. Cook the blueberry mixture over medium heat until mixture comes to a full boil. Reduce heat and cook for 5 more minutes, stirring constantly and lightly crushing berries with slotted spoon against sides of pan. Add orange zest then remove from heat. Cool for 15 to 20 minutes.

4. Pour cooled mixture into baked tart shell and chill for 30 minutes. Top with remaining blueberries and continue chilling.

5. Before serving, sift remaining 1 tablespoon powdered sugar atop tart.

child's play

Growing up, when my extended family gathered for holidays, children were usually given their own table. We missed out on the status of sitting with the adults, but we had much more fun away from the censorious grown-ups. Out of range of our parents' eyes and ears, we could fidget, misbehave, and use Goop table manners. In our island of anarchy, the behavior of cousins and friends often disintegrated into a stirring food fight.

Faced with such a reality, I designed our Fourth of July kids' table with disposable flatware, inexpensive matchstick place mats, and throwaway containers. Although other projectile food is possible, I think cherry tomatoes, strawberries, and sesame chicken fingers are particularly accurate weapons.

ADDITIONAL NOTES / INSPIRATIONS / REMEMBER NEXT YEAR

ADDITIONAL NOTES / INSPIRATIONS / REMEMBER NEXT YEAR

PEACHES

The peach season is unkind. It is much too short. It seems as if one day the peaches are green and hard, the next, perfectly ripe and succulent, the following day mushy and lying on the ground. In a panic every August, I try to capture their glorious taste in pies, ice cream, tarts, and jams. • Often the Weatherstone peach trees don't cooperate with our efforts in the kitchen. Weatherstone is at the northern limit for successful peach growing. If the cold winters don't damage the trees, the spring frosts blast the blossoms. But I am stubborn and persist in coddling the four peach trees nestled in the apple orchard. • Oddly enough, 45 minutes away, in the sheltered Hudson Valley, peaches are high art: fat, succulent, meaty, golden-sweet. The best are those grown by Doug and Talea Fincke at Montgomery Place Orchards in Annandale-on-Hudson. The Finkes have more than a dozen varieties represented in their 660 trees that extend the peach season from late July to early September. This is where I turn when my trees fail.

GOLDEN POACHED PEACHES
IN WHITE WINE MAKE A FITTING
END TO A SUMMER FEAST

I grow old . . . I grow old . . . I shall wear the bottoms of my trousers rolled. Shall I part my hair behind? Do I dare to eat a peach?

T.S. Eliot's timid Alfred Prufrock may not have thought he could survive the sensual excitement of a ripe peach, but I most assuredly can. With pleasure. No summer fruit can compete with the nectar of a tree-ripened peach. If the taste of sunlight could ever be captured, it is in the golden flesh of a juicy peach. Lately, the peach, like the tomato, has become a victim of the marketplace. It is picked before its prime and shipped to supermarkets in a state of rock-hard readiness. There is nothing to be found in these peaches. If you have a source for sun-ripened peaches, make the best of this seasonal fling. At Weatherstone, it's an affair we remember.

PEACH GALETTE
(8 Servings)

> 1 batch of Basic Tart Dough (see page 107), chilled
> 4 cups peeled, fresh peach slices, ½ inch thick
> ½ cup granulated sugar
> 2 tablespoons unsalted, chilled butter, cut into small pieces

1. Preheat oven to 375°. On a floured surface, roll out dough into a 12-inch circle. Transfer dough to an ungreased, flat baking sheet.
2. Mound peaches in the middle of the dough, spread out into an 8-inch circle. Sprinkle the peaches with sugar and dot with butter pieces.
3. Fold border of dough in onto mound of peaches, leaving the fruit in the center exposed. As you work, pinch pleats of dough to seal.
4. Bake 35 to 40 minutes or until lightly browned and bubbling.

When your meal calls for a tantalizing summer dessert but your time is limited, a peach galette, or farmer's tart, is easy to prepare and smooths the way for an after-dinner chat. I have used the hand-embroidered topiary place mats and napkins and a wicker tray to display the peach galette. The linens are fresh and simple, and they add a touch of elegance to the dessert without being too obvious.

POACHED PEACHES IN WHITE WINE
(6 Servings)

    6 ripe whole peaches
    1 bottle (750 ml.) white wine
    ½ cup cognac
    1 cup granulated sugar
    4 cups water

1. To peel peaches, dip in a large pot of boiling water for 30 seconds then place in cold water for one minute. Peel skins.

2. Combine wine, cognac, sugar, and water in a large saucepan: bring to a boil. Lower heat and simmer for 5 minutes. Add peaches and cook, uncovered, over low heat for 20 minutes, or until peaches are tender. Remove peaches and place in bowl.

3. Over medium heat, briskly simmer poaching liquid until reduced by half, approximately 30 minutes. Strain liquid into bowl of peaches and refrigerate for 1 to 2 hours before serving.

*personal notes:*_____

_____

_____

PEACH CRISP
(6 Servings)

    1 tabelspoon, plus 1 stick unsalted butter, chilled
    5 cups peeled, fresh peach slices, ½ inch thick
    1¼ cups all-purpose flour
    1 cup granulated sugar
    1 teaspoon ground cinnamon
    ¼ teaspoon salt

1. Preheat oven to 375°. Using 1 tablespoon of butter, grease 2-quart ovenproof dish or 8-by-8-inch pan. Place peach slices in prepared pan.

2. In a medium bowl, whisk together flour, sugar, cinnamon and salt. Dice remaining 1 stick of butter into small pieces and add to flour mixture. With a pastry cutter or two knives, work butter into dry ingredients until butter is incorporated and the mixture is crumbly; do not overwork.

3. Evenly layer mixture over peaches and bake for approximately 30 to 35 minutes or until bubbly and topping is browned. Serve hot.

PEACH SHORTCAKE
(6 Servings)

2¾ cups flour
4 teaspoons baking powder
½ teaspoon salt
½ teaspoon cream of tartar
¾ cup plus 2½ tablespoon granulated sugar
1 stick unsalted butter, chilled and diced into small pieces
⅔ cup milk
1 large egg yolk, lightly beaten
½ teaspoon pure vanilla extract
1 cup heavy cream, chilled
3 to 4 tablespoons Grand Marnier
4 cups fresh peaches, peeled, pitted and sliced ½-inch thick

1. Preheat oven to 375°. Sift together the flour, baking powder, salt, cream of tartar and 3 tablespoons sugar. Using a pastry cutter or two knives, work butter into flour until mixture resembles coarse corn meal. Add milk, egg yolk and vanilla and with a rubber spatula, stir and press all ingredients together. Dough should be soft but not sticky.

2. Turn dough onto a floured surface and gently knead 5 times to incorporate ingredients and form a ball; do not overwork. Press dough into an even ¾-inch thickness. Use a 3-inch biscuit cutter to form rounds and place on an ungreased flat baking sheet. Gather scraps, pat out and cut more rounds to make a total of 6 biscuits.

3. Brush tops of biscuits with a small amount of chilled cream (return remaining cream to the refrigerator) and sprinkle each with about ¼ teaspoon of sugar. Bake until lightly browned, about 12 to 15 minutes.

4. Meanwhile, in a medium bowl, add ½ cup sugar and Grand Marnier to the peach slices, toss to coat and allow to macerate at room temperature.

5. Beat remaining heavy cream and remaining 2 tablespoons sugar with an electric mixer until soft peaks form. When biscuits have cooled, slice in half horizontally and layer with peaches and whipped cream. Serve immediately.

TIP

THE RIPEST PEACH:
- *The amount of red blush on a peach depends on the variety and is not always a sign of ripeness. Better signs of ripeness are a well-defined crease and a strong "peachy" scent.*
- *Peaches picked too early will never gain in sweetness if ripened indoors. The riper a peach is at harvest time, the more sugar it will contain.*
- *Once a mature peach begins to ripen it never stops, but you can slow the rate of ripening by storing mature peaches in the refrigerator.*

I love the decadence of warm peach shortcake, above, piled high with luscious whipped cream. I also use generous scoops of vanilla and chocolate ice cream from the local dairy to top our peach crisp, *(right)*.

THE MARRIAGE
OF
REBECCA AND SAM
AUGUST 13, 1999

Zucchini and Curry Soup
•
Poached Salmon
with a green herb mayonaise
•
Orzo with Summer Vegetables
•
Mesclun Salad with Feta

A SUMMER WEDDING

Recently, a young friend came to me knowing of my love of flowers and asked me to suggest a decorating scheme for a small outdoor August wedding. Wanting to veer from the traditional virginal white, she asked if I could recommend a plan incorporating the vibrant colors of a wild summer garden. I took the bait; the inspiration was right before me. What better time and place for a late summer wedding than when the cutting and vegetable garden is peaking with a full spectrum of color? Although I devised flower arrangements to showcase happy yellow sunflowers, heavenly blue hydrangeas, and shocking pink cosmos and zinnias, I needed a color combination that would unite all the vibrant colors. I settled on a simple repeating melody of blue and white. Blue-and-white checked gingham became the clothes for the luncheon tables, as well as the fabric for the bridesmaids' and flower girls' dresses.

An antique blue-and-white quilt that had been hiding in storage covered the homemade altar. The ceremony took place under an old wooden pergola festooned with swags of borrowed annuals from the cutting garden.

Garden benches decorated with a handful of flowers gathered with a raffia bow were transformed into pews for the small garden wedding. The flowers were tied on at the eleventh hour so they did not have to withstand the summer heat. The pergola flower clusters were built on floral foam forms, which prolonged their life span, then were linked together to create the effect of a garland. The huge centerpiece basket of flowers provided the focal point of the ceremony. This wedding theme is easily adaptable to any summer celebration, from a birthday to a festive summer dance.

HOW TO MAKE THE PERGOLA DECORATION

Tools for Each Section:

    Rectangular caged floral foam blocks (found in wholesale
      floral supply catalogues, craft stores or flower districts)
    Small plastic floral vials filled with water
    Pruners
    Hammer and nails

Flowers Used (All flowers approximately 6-inches long):

    Two different sizes of sunflowers
    Blue mophead hydrangeas
    White and pink cosmos
    Pink, orange, and yellow zinnias
    Marigolds
    Stock

How-To:

Thoroughly soak floral foam forms in water (treated with a few drops of chlorine bleach), then drain well.

Start the arrangement by placing the largest flowers into the oasis block: first, hydrangeas, then sunflowers, followed by marigolds, zinnias, and stock.

Place clusters of cosmos inside the water vials before putting them into the foam so that the delicate stems won't break and the flowers are given added height and pronunciation.

Consider gravity when doing the arrangement. Sunflowers are very heavy and cumbersome and may fall out of the arrangement if placed facing downward. Also, heavier flowers will be more secure if placed on the top of the cage rather than on the sides.

After you have finished your arrangement, nail or wire to pews, walls, or wherever they will be displayed. Once the arrangements are in place, add any leftover flowers you need for balance.

I asked cake artist Sylvia Weinstock, to make a wedding cake that copied a terra-cotta pot filled with the flowers I had used in the bouquets. When the cake arrived, I was astounded at how close she came in color and in style to my flowers. Where do the live flowers stop and the cake begin?

Sylvia Weinstock's talent is at its fullest when she is given the challenge of creating a flowerpot cake filled with sugar flowers. The flowers at the base of the pot are real. The ones on top are Sylvia's creation. The flowers bounce off the simple blue-and-white gingham tablecloth, which, in addition to the flowers, inspired the gift wrappings. Reiterating the theme in the wrapped gifts makes the overall impact stronger. I use live flowers on packages; when I know that they will not have a long wait, I merely tie the flowers on. I also try to use flowers that do not instantly wilt. If it is an easily perishable flower, I hide a small floral water pick under the bow. Be careful that your pick is airtight; otherwise, you will end up with a wet package.

CORN

I think I can safely say that sweet corn is one of the few vegetables that tastes better today than it did in my rose-colored childhood memories. The corn of my Missouri youth would turn from sugar to starch the minute it was picked, so the maxim stood: Gardeners shouldn't pick their hybrid or open-pollinated corn until the water was boiling on the stove. Although this saw still lingers, the newer hybrid sugar-enhanced and supersweets hold on to their sugar until the boiling water and the cook are ready. • As a child, I always checked to see if "the corn was as high as an elephant's eye by the 4th of July." It never was. In the colder New England climate that is my home now, sweet corn can rarely be harvested before the end of July. The farmers here, as elsewhere, plant in two-week cycles that extend the sweet corn season through August. At Weatherstone we plant 'Starshine,' a mid-season white corn that ripens about two weeks later than the earliest varieties available, but is well worth the wait. • To take maximum advantage of the season, we use corn in a variety of ways, fresh and frozen. My favorite is still on the cob, drenched with melted butter. (Forget fat-free fashion. No butter, no corn, as far as I am concerned. . . . My record is nine ears in one sitting) Frozen corn is only a reminder of its summer self, but it tides over the corn fanatic in me until I can sink my teeth into that first ear of the season, and with the butter dripping down my chin, say "At last it's really summer."

There are probably more opinions about the proper cooking of corn on the cob than there are varieties. We respect these time-honored traditions, but there are a few rules to apply whether you are steaming, roasting, or boiling.

• Older varieties of corn needed longer cooking, but the new hybrid sweets are more tender. Two minutes of boiling or steaming is enough to bring out their flavor. The longer the sugar-enhanced corns are cooked, the tougher they become and the more the sugar turns to starch.

• Adding a cup of milk or a pinch of sugar to the boiling water doesn't sweeten just-picked corn, but it may help improve the flavor of supermarket corn.

• Don't salt the water. Salt in the cooking water toughens the kernels.

• Always roast corn with the husks on and silk removed. Soak the husks in cold water for a few minutes to keep them from burning. Roast about 4 inches above the coals, or bury the cobs in the hot coals, for about 15 minutes.

• To roast corn in the oven, remove husks and silk. Rub the ears with butter, salt, and pepper. Wrap each ear in foil and bake at 400° for about 15 minutes.

• Microwave with husks on and silks removed for about 6 minutes on high.

NANCY QUATTRINI'S CORN CHOWDER RECIPE
(6 to 8 Servings)

4 tablespoons unsalted butter
1 medium onion, chopped
1 red pepper, chopped
1 yellow pepper, chopped
2 stalks celery, chopped
4 cups fresh corn kernels
4 cups potatoes, cubed
5½ cups chicken stock
½ cup heavy cream
½ cup fresh dill, finely chopped

1. Melt buffer in a large pot over medium heat. Add onion, red and yellow peppers and celery and sauté 10 minutes or until onions are translucent and slightly golden. Add corn and potatoes and sauté for an additional 10 minutes, stirring occasionally.

2. Add chicken stock, cover and bring to a boil. Reduce heat and simmer, uncovered for 25 to 30 minutes or until potatoes are tender.

3. As potatoes begin to soften, use a slotted spoon to partially crush potatoes against the sides of the pan to thicken broth. Add cream and dill and serve.

ROASTED CORN JALAPEÑO MUFFINS
(Makes 12 Muffins)

2 medium ears fresh corn, husked
2 teaspoons plus ¼ cup canola oil
1½ cups all-purpose flour
¼ cup stone-ground corn meal
¼ cup granulated sugar
2 teaspoons baking powder
½ teaspoon salt
1 cup milk at room temperature
2 large eggs, slightly beaten
1 fresh jalapeño pepper, seeded and finely minced
¼ cup grated cheddar cheese

1. Preheat oven to 400°. Grease muffin tin with 1 teaspoon oil and set aside.

2. To roast corn, place ears on a baking sheet greased with 1 teaspoon oil. Roast in a preheated oven for 30 minutes, turning ears every 10 minutes. Cool slightly and cut kernels off cob to equal 1 cup roasted corn.

3. In a large mixing bowl, whisk together flour, corn meal, sugar, baking powder and salt. Add milk, eggs, jalapeño and remaining ¼ cup oil. Stir until just blended.

4. Fold in roasted corn and cheese. Divide batter evenly among muffin cups but not more than ⅔ full.

5. Bake for 20 to 25 minutes until golden.

CORN SOUFFLÉ
WITH HERB CHEESE SAUCE
(4 Servings)

    4 tablespoons unsalted butter
1½ teaspoons granulated sugar
    ½ teaspoon finely chopped habañero pepper
    2 tablespoons all-purpose flour
    1 cup cold milk
    3 large eggs at room temperature, separated
    1 cup grated Vermont cheddar cheese
    1 teaspoon salt
    ¼ teaspoon ground white pepper
    2 cups fresh corn kernels

1. Preheat oven to 350°. Using 1 tablespoon butter, grease four 4-inch soufflé dishes. Dust bottom and sides lightly with sugar and set aside.

2. Melt remaining 3 tablespoons butter in sauté pan over low heat and add habañero. Sauté for 2 minutes. Add flour and stir for about 1 minute.

3. Slowly add milk, ¼ cup at a time, stirring constantly, and simmer for about 3 minutes or until thick. Add cheese and continue to cook, stirring until cheese melts and batter is smooth.

4. In a small bowl, lightly beat egg yolks then add approximately ¼ cup of the hot corn batter. Pour yolk mixture into the rest of the batter in pan and cook for 1 minute. Remove from heat and allow to cool slightly.

5. In a medium bowl, beat egg whites with an electric mixer or whisk until stiff but not dry. Gently fold egg whites into corn batter just until combined.

6. Divide evenly among prepared soufflé dishes, place on baking sheet and bake for 20 to 25 minutes, or until lightly browned on top. Do not open the oven to check soufflés before 20 minutes have elapsed. Serve immediately with Herb Cheese Sauce.

Herb Cheese Sauce
(Makes 2¼ cups)

    2 tablespoons unsalted butter
    4 tablespoons finely chopped shallots
    3 tablespoons flour
2½ cups cold milk
1½ cups grated Vermont cheddar cheese
    2 tablespoons chopped fresh basil
    1 tablespoons chopped fresh oregano
    1 tablespoon chopped fresh tarragon
    1 tablespoon chopped ftesh mint

1. In a sauté pan over medium heat, melt butter and sauté shallots until transparent, about 2 to 3 minutes. Add flour, reduce heat to low and cook for 2 minutes while continuing to stir.

2. Add milk slowly, ¼ cup at a time, stirring constantly. Cook until smooth, about 2 minutes.

3. Add grated cheese while stirring and cook until creamy, about 3 minutes. Remove from heat and add fresh chopped herbs. Serve warm with corn soufflé.

TIP

HOW TO FREEZE CORN
- *Husk corn. Blanche ears for one minute in boiling water.*
- *Plunge ears into ice water.*
- *Stand ears on a cookie sheet and cut off kernels.*
- *Pack in freezer bags and put in freezer.*

HOT
FLOWERS

By the time late summer comes to Weatherstone, the perennial garden has had its say. The peonies are history, the delphiniums have browned and dropped their petals, and the full flush of roses is over. The subtle shades of purple, lilac, pink, white, and silver-green, so touted by William Robinson and Gertrude Jekyll, have expired in the August heat. • I do not mourn the passing perennials because waiting in the potager are the riotously colored annuals. Zinnias, cosmos, rudbeckia, sunflowers, hollyhocks, coreopsis, marigolds, and nasturtiums boldly take over with their arresting fuchsias, sunshine yellows, flaming reds, magentas, and electric oranges. • I initially isolated these vibrant "hot" flowers in the cutting and vegetable garden to avoid a clash with the paler blossoms in the perennial borders. The pairing worked; I found that the hot colors popped when juxtaposed with the primary colors in the vegetable garden. The annuals naturally segued into the house: orange nasturtiums keep company with scarlet mini tomatoes and chartreuse apples heighten the appeal of crimson zinnias. Zinnias are the troopers of my cutting garden, never failing to strive for extreme vigor in color and stamina. • Often zinnias are put down by garden snobs as being pedestrian, too easy, too eager. While they may not be as glamorous as the lofty perennials, their exuberant color and size more than make up for a lack of horticultural pedigree. I love all these hardworking, heavy-producing annuals. I cannot consider summer complete without them.

f From July to mid-September, the flowers that come into my house are culled from the cutting garden. Here, I have no worries about disturbing the harmony of the perennial borders; this garden was planted for picking. The annual flowers chosen for the cutting garden are assigned a dual purpose. Most important, they must fulfill my desire for heightened color. I look for the primary colors of red, blue, and yellow to play off their complements of green, orange, and purple. Analogous color combinations of red, yellow, and orange—best exhibited by marigolds, zinnias, cosmos, and sunflower—are some of my favorites. But the plants also need to hold their own in the garden even though their heads are constantly being robbed. Temperamental horticultural specimens won't do here. Fortunately, most annuals like this form of pruning. By clipping them for the vase, I am essentially deadheading and preventing seed formation. The happy annuals respond by continuing to bloom until the first frost.

personal notes:

A riotous wave of 'Bright Lights Mix' cosmos blooms by midsummer. Coupled with zinnias, the cosmos are invaluable cut flowers. The constant deadheading to keep them producing is a time-consuming task, but I enjoy the Zen-like repetition. Deadheading has become my most prized early morning chore.

TIP

Make deadheading a daily ritual. Attach a small pair of stainless-steel scissors to a ribbon, slip the ribbon around your neck, and snip fading flower buds as you stroll. When you come in from the garden, hang the scissors on a doorknob or other convenient spot for the next day's deadheading.

YELLOW TONES LIGHT UP THE
CUTTING GARDEN WITH
FLECKS OF SUNSHINE

Yellow is the most vivid of all colors; it demands attention. It is the first color the human eye notices. Think of a yellow caution sign, a child in a yellow slicker, or a yellow taxi. Yellow has the same effect in the garden, it wakes up your brain. When yellow takes center stage, the effect can be intoxicating. Wide rivers of naturalized daffodils inspire giddiness, a brilliant burst of foolish yellow after the somber grays of winter.

Given yellow's egoistic properties, it is a color that should be used sparingly in the perennial border or it will hog the visual spectrum. Traditionally, the classic English border of silver pink and lavender accommodates a certain amount of soft yellow for good balance. But other than a dash of pale butter, I am not a lover of yellow in the perennial border. This is not the case in the cutting garden. The brilliant yellows of sunflowers, coreopsis, rudbeckia, cosmos, zinnias, and marigolds predominate in the cutting beds at Weatherstone and are essential elements of simple summer bouquets.

If an arrangement is looking flat, I pop in a few yellow flowers and the bouquet is lit by a fleck of sunshine. I sometimes use yellow flowers by themselves, but more often than not, I use yellow as a pointillist painter would, as punctuation. As you can see on the following page, yellow is especially effective in electrifying a backdrop of cobalt blue.

From top left: The two sunflowers with their rich chocolate-brown centers are standouts in the cutting garden, as are rudbeckia 'Irish Eyes,' so aptly named with their green centers.

The vibrant yellow sunflowers and electric blue *Hydrangea macrophylla* replicate clear blue skies and bright summer sun. On the rainiest day, they brighten the entire breakfast room. Small blue glass vases of *Coreopsis tinctoria* are appreciated for the carefree attitude they bring to the morning table. The small cobalt juice glasses filled with *Sanvitalia procumbens*, with their dark brown centers, offer a Lilliputian echo of the sunflowers in the large arrangement.

with blue

personal notes:

oranges

Orange is a color that begs to be appreciated in bright sunshine. When I was working as a designer, combinations of vibrant orange, saffron yellow and chartreuse always served as an inspiration for my summer and resort collections. I ignored orange for winter designs since it has the unfortunate ability to make some complexions look sallow. Orange needs a canvas of sun-bronzed skin in order to project what color theorists say orange evokes: fire and flames, lust, vigor, excitement and adventure. If the color theorists are right, it sounds to me like a bouquet filled with fervent orange annuals could be the start of a very interesting summer.

From top left: 'Candy Cane Mix' zinnia, 'Whirlybird Mix' nasturtium and a young 'Golden Dawn' zinnia are some of my favorite orange annuals. *Opposite:* A table set with orange linens against a backdrop of summer green is the perfect foil for a Majolica vase filled with hot-colored zinnias.

'Scarlet Flame' zinnia

Tomato 'Sweet 100'

'Candy Cane Mix' zinnia

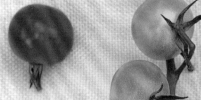

'Golden Climax' marigold

'Golden Dawn' zinnia

Viburnum berries

'Golden State' zinnia

Hot oranges come together to play off the tones of the majolica vase and the Coke bottle green glasses.

A FULL SPECTRUM OF SUNSHINE
FROM BUTTER YELLOW TO
RUSSET ORANGE SATURATES
A SUMMER TABLE

We grow 'Whirlybird Mix' nasturtiums for bouquets because they flower in a wide range of colors, from butter yellow to coral to a full spectrum of orange, scarlet, and russet.

pinks

I may be pilloried by some political sisters for saying so, but I think pink is the most feminine of colors. Images go through my mind that run the spectrum from innocent little girls in pearl pink tutus to the sizzling tartiness of a hot pink Schiaperelli dress. I vividly remember a trip to India, seeing the women of Rajistan walking along the roadsides in bare feet, their brown ankles bound in gold bracelets. As they walked, they swirled their skirts of fushcia and orange in the hot sun. I had never considered the possiblilities of mating orange with pink until that day. Now it is one of my favorite summer color combinations, well represented in the cutting garden. Zinnias and cosmos are the heavyweights, coming on strong with a full array of pinks from chalky rose to magenta to raspberry to carmine to brilliant fuschia. Although the balance of tint and hue is important when mixing pink, Mother Nature is a great guideline. She offers a pink that works with a whole array of colors so each of these pinks can find a complementary companion.

As a cut flower, zinnias and cosmos are invaluable. *From top left:* Cosmos 'Radiance' meshes well with my favorite zinnias such as 'Bright Pink,' 'Pink Splendor,' 'Bonita Red,' 'Purple Prince,' and 'Scarlet Flame.'

A SUMMER BIRTHDAY PARTY

Although the perennial border has peaked by August, and the bugs are at their fiercest, outdoor celebrations cannot be ignored. The deep green ferny foliage makes a perfect backdrop for the bossy red, pink, and coral zinnias. The Toile de Jouy tablecloth in green and white, and the bottle green benches, make a simple palette from which to highlight my best zinnia crop in years. Some may say that this is not much of an achievement. Gardening perfectionists often put zinnias at the bottom of the horticultural food chain. I ignore this sentiment and plant twenty-two different zinnia varieties. After much trial and error, I have eliminated most of the miniature zinnias and now focus on the largest blossoms in the boldest colors.

I've been collecting gift wrapping paper and ribbons from around the world for more than twenty years. When the time comes to dress a gift, I have a large palette to draw from. I found this hand-printed paper in Venice (it is now widely available here in art stores) and the silk ribbon in Paris. I've drawn from the green of the Toile de Jouy tablecloth to coordinate the colors using a similar value of green but relying on different textures and intensities. The pale, icy green Venetian glass makes any drink seem refreshing because of the delicate, clear color.

personal notes:

THROW CAUTION TO THE WIND WITH A
SATISFYING EXPLOSION OF COLOR

From top right: Mainstays of the mixed bouquet include 'Daydream' (pale pink) and 'Pinkie' (magenta) cosmos, 'Bright Pink,' 'Crimson Monarch,' and 'Scarlet Flame' zinnias and 'Bright Lights Mix' cosmos.

What fun it is to throw caution to the wind! Take every vibrant annual and throw them into a vase and you will find that all the colors of the cutting garden come together in a satisfying explosion of color. Mix away! Don't be shy. It is hard to go wrong as long as you don't err on the side of cold conservatism. Viburnum berries from the garden hedges support *Coreopsis tinctoria,* cosmos 'Bright Lights Mix,' 'Ladybird Scarlet,' 'Pinkie,' and 'Dazzler.' 'Envy,' 'Crimson Monarch,' and 'Scarlet Flame' zinnias are tucked in among the cosmos. Purple loosestrife—not the detested invader of wetlands, but a tamer cultivar—pokes through the top of the arrangement, balancing the effect of the berries. The bouquet becomes the focal point for a relaxed summer luncheon table draped with a blue-and-white bistro tablecloth.

personal notes: _____

Seed companies such as Thompson & Morgan have recently started selling more separate-color seed packs of annual flowers, rather than the more common XYZ mix. I have taken advantage of this trend and started many of my own annuals in the hoophouses. By starting from seed and buying single-color six-packs at the nursery, it has been easier to control color in the garden and in bouquets.

RED
'Dazzler' cosmos
'Ladybird Scarlet' cosmos
'Versaille Carmine' cosmos
'Empress of India' nasturtium
'Bonita Red' zinnia
'Crimson Monarch' zinnia
'Halo' zinnia
'Meteor' zinnia
'Righteous Red' zinnia
'Scarlet Flame' zinnia
'Scarlet Splendor' zinnia

DARK RED/BURGUNDY
'Chocolate' cosmos
'The Watchman' hollyhock
'Whirlybird Mix' nasturtium
'Ace of Spades' scabiosa
'Black Prince' snapdragon
'Chianti' sunflower
'Prado Red' sunflower

MAGENTA
'Radiance' cosmos
'Versailles' cosmos
'Royal Purple' zinnia

PINK
'Daydream' cosmos
'Pinkie' cosmos
'Sonata Fairy Mix' cosmos
'Versailles Blush Pink' cosmos
'Versailles Pink' cosmos
'Bright Pink' zinnia
'Exquisite' zinnia
'Pink Splendor' zinnia

ORANGE
'Bright Lights' cosmos
'Toreador' marigold
'Whirlybird Mix' nasturtium
'Double Gold' rudbeckia
'Irish Eyes' rudbeckia
'Autumn Beauty' sunflower
'Golden State' zinnia

PURPLE
'Finest Mix' scabiosa
'Purple Prince' zinnia

YELLOW
'Sunburst' coreopsis
'Sunray' coreopsis
Coreopsis tinctoria
'Kid Stuff' sunflower
'Mammoth' sunflower
'Prado Yellow' sunflower
'Tiger Eye' sunflower

YELLOW-ORANGE
Black-eyed Susan
'Golden Climax' marigold
'Whirlybird Mix' nasturtium
'Mandarin Orange' sanvitalia
'Supermane' sunflower
'Tangina' sunflower
'Taiyo' sunflower

YELLOW-GREEN
'Envy' zinnia

RED-ORANGE
'Inferno' eschscholtzia

VARIEGATED
'Candy Cane Mix' zinnia

GARDEN JOURNAL

DATE: --

GARDEN LOCATION: --

PLANTS: --

COMMENTS / RESULTS: --

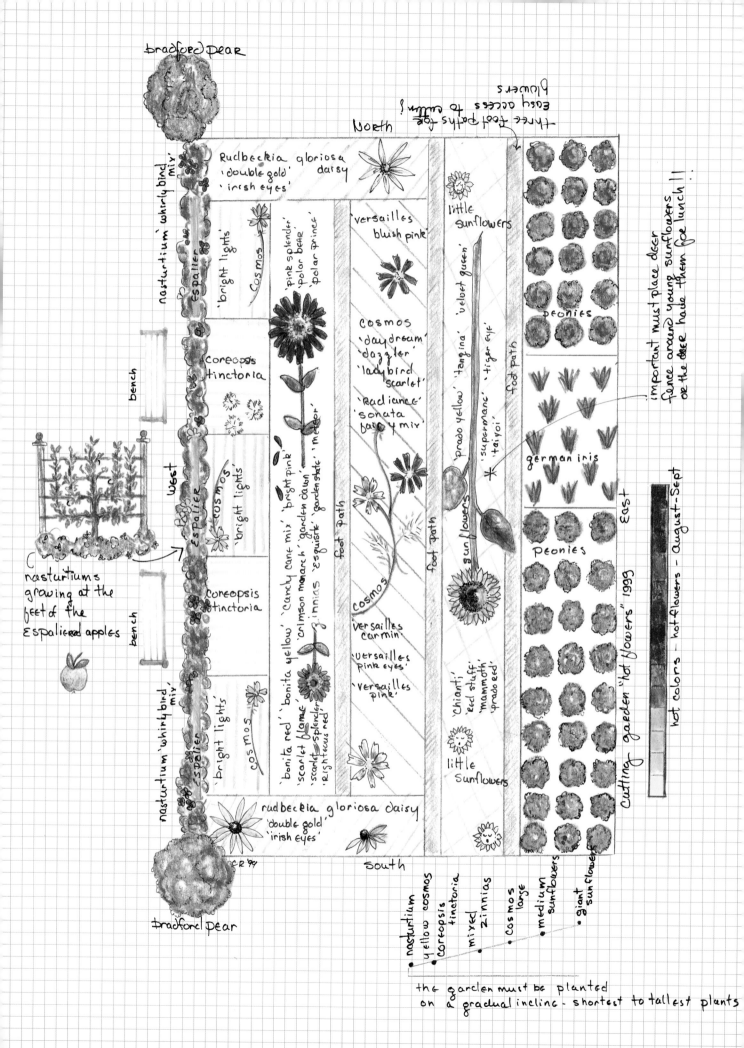

bradford pear

Rudbeckia gloriosa daisy
'double gold'
'irish eyes'

North

Easy access to cutting
flowers

three foot paths for
flowers

nasturtium 'whirly bird' mix'

espalier

'bright lights'
Cosmos

coreopsis
tinctoria

West

espalier

Cosmos
'bright lights'

bench

bench

nasturtiums
growing at the
feet of the
Espaliered apples

coreopsis
tinctoria

'bright lights'
cosmos

nasturtium 'whirly bird' mix'

espalier

rudbeckia gloriosa daisy
'double gold'
'irish eyes'

CR 99

South

'pink splendor'
'polar bear'
'polar prince'

cosmos
'daydream'
'dazzler'
'ladybird
scarlet'
'radiance'
sonata
daisy mix'

versailles
blush pink

cosmos

versailles
carmin

'versailles
pink eyes'

'versailles
pink'

'bonita red' 'bonita yellow' 'candy cane mix' 'bright pink'
'scarlet flame' 'crimson monarch' 'garden dawn'
'scarlet splendor' 'garden shade' 'meteor'
'righteous red' zinnias 'esquiste

foot path

foot path

little
sunflowers

'prado yellow' 'tangina' 'velvet queen'

'supemane' 'tiger eye'
'taiyoi'

sunflowers

'chianti'
'red stuff'
'mammoth'
'prado red'

little
sunflowers

foot path

peonies

german iris

peonies

East

important must place deer
fence around young sunflowers
or the deer have them for lunch!!

hot colors - hot flowers - August-Sept

Cutting garden "hot flowers" 1999

bradford pear

nasturtium
yellow cosmos
coreopsis
tinctoria
mixed
zinnias
Cosmos
large
medium
sunflowers
giant
sunflowers

the garden must be planted
on a gradual incline - shortest to tallest plants

TOMATOES

Tomatoes do seem to bring out the braggarts in us all. Gardeners who are humble about the flowering of their double trilliums get pretty puffed-up about the first birth of a ripe tomato. The cutoff date for kudos is the Fourth of July; those above the Mason-Dixon Line, if you can get a tomato to ripen before the fireworks appear, then add a notch to your horticultural belt. Unfortunately, the flavor of most of the early-ripening varieties (or varieties bred for cold tolerance), doesn't have the citric zing of the sun-soaked beefsteaks. But any home-grown tomato is superior to the taste-less clods found in today's supermarkets. • I have taken myself out of the ripening race because I am unwilling to bring out the big guns: black plastic mulch. It may keep the tomato plant's roots warm and cozy, but it looks like widow's weeds in the potager. For early and ornamental fruit, I depend on a prolific sure thing: 'Sweet Tangerine,' 'Yellow Pear' and 'Supersweet 100' cherry tomatoes. They present a temptation to anyone walking on the grass path next to the potager: Pick me. Pick me.

PRESERVING THE TOMATO HARVEST

By the end of August, the Weatherstone kitchen is piled high with wicker baskets full of ripe tomatoes. I go tomato mad for weeks, devising every possible culinary permutation, but the vines keep pumping out more fruit. Not being able to bear the sight of a rotting tomato, I know I should take out the canning equipment and put up pints of tomato sauce, but time is against me.

A few summers ago, Margarida, with her Portuguese pragmatism, took the glut into her own hands and conducted an experiment. She gathered a dozen whole, fresh, unblemished tomatoes at the peak of ripeness, popped them into a zippered plastic bag and tossed them in the freezer. Strangely enough, the fruit didn't mind a bit. Now, in winter, whenever we need chopped tomatoes, I take a couple of tomatoes out of the freezer bag and thaw them. When unfrozen, the skins slip right off and the pulp is ready to be added to pasta sauce, stews, or soup.

If you have the climate, another way of coping with a bountiful tomato harvest is to dry them in the sun. This is a tricky business. The temperature must be above 85° and there must be less than 60 percent relative humidity for this method to work. Select the best plum tomatoes (they are less watery). Wash the tomatoes and cut them in half lengthwise. Place the halves cut side down on a nylon or plastic screen window. Cover the tomatoes with one layer of cheesecloth to protect the tomatoes from dirt and insects. Tent the cheesecloth slightly with short glasses to increase air circulation. Place the screen outside in direct sun, but bring it indoors overnight to avoid the dew. Turn the tomatoes halfway through the drying process (it may take two or three days for the tomatoes to dry).

Store sun-dried tomatoes dry, in sterilized glass jars with tight-fitting lids. Alternatively, you can dry plum tomato halves in an electric food dryer set at 120° for about twenty-four hours. Drying tomatoes in a conventional oven is difficult because you must maintain a low heat of 120° consistently for twenty-four hours.

To reconstitute the dried tomatoes, pour boiling water over them, then let them sit for five minutes, or until they soften. Drain and cover with olive oil seasoned with a garlic clove. Marinate the tomatoes for twenty-four hours in the refrigerator. The tomatoes can be stored in the oil, if refrigerated, for two to three weeks. Reconstituted tomatoes also can be puréed with their olive oil and used as you would tomato paste.

personal notes: _____

_____

_____

'Sungold'

'Red Currant'

'Costoluto Genovese'

'San Marzano'

'Roma'

'Early Girl'

TIP

Tomatoes and peppers love calcium. Put two
Tums in the bottom of the planting hole. Really.
The calcium not only prevents blossom end rot,
but gives the plant a boost. A teaspoon of
Epsom salts or a few crushed eggshells will
also do the trick.

A TOMATO CENTERPIECE SURROUNDED BY BASIL FILLS THE AIR WITH A RICH LICORICE AROMA

Tomatoes, onions, garlic and olive oil—the staples of the Weatherstone kitchen—join dill and chicken stock for Tomato-Dill Soup (*below*) served hot or chilled. A dollop of sour cream can be added for those not frightened of calories.

TOMATO-DILL SOUP
(Makes About 3 Cups★)

2 tablespoons olive oil
3 cups chopped onions
5 cups chopped fresh tomatoes
Salt and pepper to taste
1 teaspoon ground sage
1 bay leaf
One 12-ounce can of tomato purée
½ cup heavy cream, chilled
¾ cup chopped fresh dill

1. Add olive oil to a large pan over medium heat and sauté onions until soft and slightly golden, about 7 minutes.
2. Add tomatoes, salt, pepper, sage, bay leaf, and tomato purée and simmer, covered, for 20 minutes.
3. Working in small batches, push mixture through a sieve with a rubber spatula into a medium-sized bowl; discard solids. Chill purée in refrigerator.
4. One hour before serving, whisk in cream and dill. Continue chilling and serve cold.

★This is a rich soup; small portions are recommended

*personal notes:*_____

_____

The late summer kitchen at Weatherstone is overwhelmed with orange and red tomatoes. To celebrate the first harvest (and to lessen the tomato burden), I dressed the luncheon table with the best picks and coupled them with sprigs of licorice-scented basil. Diners who would never consider decimating a floral centerpiece were not shy about picking at the sweet cherry tomatoes or pinching leaves from the basil, closing their eyes as they breathed in the aroma. The simple table settings and speedy table arrangement left plenty of time for kitchen preparation. The lunch hinged on a puréed Tomato-Dill soup, but your first-harvest luncheon could include any recipe derived from fresh yellow, orange, red, purple, or striped tomatoes.

MOZZARELLA, TOMATO AND PINE NUT TART
(8 Servings)

6 fresh plum tomatoes, halved lengthwise
½ cup grated Parmesan cheese
1 tart crust, unbaked (see Basic Tart Dough recipe, p.107)
2 medium fresh tomatoes, seeded and diced
¼ cup chopped fresh basil
½ pound fresh mozzarella, thinly sliced or grated
⅓ cup pine nuts, lightly toasted
1 teaspoon red pepper flakes (optional)

1. Preheat oven to 225°. Place plum tomatoes, cut side up on a flat baking sheet and roast for 3 hours. Remove from oven. Cool and set aside. Reset oven to 375°.
2. Place tart shell on baking sheet and bake for 15 minutes. Remove from oven and cool.
3. Sprinkle ¼ cup Parmesan cheese on bottom of cooled crust. Layer fresh tomatoes over Parmesan then sprinkle with basil. Place mozzarella over basil then place roasted tomato halves on top.
4. Sprinkle with pine nuts, red pepper flakes and remaining Parmesan cheese. Bake for 20 to 25 minutes or until cheese melts. Serve warm or at room temperature.

INDIVIDUAL JALAPEÑO AND TOMATO TARTS
(8 Servings)

8 unbaked 4-inch tart shells, chilled (see Basic Tart Dough recipe)
1 tablespoon olive oil
3 fresh jalapeño peppers, seeded and finely chopped
4 cloves garlic, finely chopped
Two (4-ounce) cans chopped mild green chilies
Pinch of salt
2 cups grated smoked gruyere cheese
1 medium yellow (and/or red) tomato, sliced ¼-inch thick
¼ cup chopped fresh parsley
2 tablespoons chopped fresh cilantro

1. Preheat oven to 375° Place tart shells on flat baking sheet and bake for 10 minutes, then set aside to cool. Reset oven to 400°.
2. In a small sauté pan, heat olive oil and sauté jalapeño and garlic over medium heat for 2 minutes. Add salt, green chilies and sauté for 3 more minutes. Remove from heat.
3. Sprinkle 2 tablespoons of cheese in bottom of each tart shell. Top with 2 tablespoons chili mixture, then layer with remaining cheese. Arrange tomato slices on top of tarts and sprinkle with parsley and cilantro.
4. Bake for 20 to 25 minutes or until the cheese melts. Serve either hot or at room temperature.

CAROLYNE'S FRESH TOMATO SAUCE
(Makes About 2 Cups)

2 tablespoons butter
¼ cup olive oil
6 to 8 cloves garlic, minced
1 medium onion, chopped
½ cup red wine
4 cups chopped tomatoes
Salt and pepper to taste
½ teaspoon red pepper flakes
3 tablespoons capers
½ cup fresh basil, julienned

1. Add butter and olive oil to a large skillet. Over medium heat, sauté garlic and onions until translucent, about 3 minutes.

2. Add wine, simmer briskly for 3 or 4 minutes to reduce sauce by half.

3. Add chopped tomatoes, salt, pepper, and red pepper flakes. Reduce heat to medium low and simmer uncovered for 15 to 20 minutes, stirring occasionally.

4. Remove sauce from heat and stir in capers and basil. Toss with pasta, such as linguine or spaghetti.

BASIC TART DOUGH RECIPE
(Makes Eight 4-Inch Tarts or One 8- to 10-Inch Tart)

1¼ cup flour
1 stick unsalted butter, chilled and cut into small dice
Pinch of salt
2 to 3 tablespoon ice water

1. Put flour and salt into the bowl of a food processor and pulse 3 times to blend. Add butter, lightly toss with your fingers to coat pieces with flour. Pulse processor about 8 times to cut in butter. Dough should resemble coarse corn meal and butter pieces should be no larger than small peas.

2. Add ice water gradually by tablespoon through feed tube while pulsing machine. Dough will begin to pull together into a ball.

3. Remove dough from processor, shape into a disk, sprinkle lightly with flour, and wrap in wax paper. Refrigerate until ready to roll out for tarts and pies.

TOMATO AND ONION SALAD

Red onion rings and tomato slices make a quick salad when sprinkled with white balsamic vinegar, salt and pepper, and garnished with fresh basil.

HYDRANGEAS

One of the perversities of life is that we always want what we can't have. Southern gardeners may envy my growing zone because our winters are cold enough to suit the hibernating delphinium as a perennial. I, in turn, envy Zone 6 gardeners because their climate is good to Hydrangea macrophylla. Neither of us can have both. • Although I successfully grow hedges of cream Hydrangea paniculata, it's the blue and lavender mopheads that are the focus of my covetousness. The only way I can have them is as a cut flower. So I am left to raiding friends' gardens in Southampton or driving to the New York flower markets to fill my vases. On a recent trip to California, I made a beeline for a Malibu grower who claims that the coastal climate provides perfect growing conditions for hydrangea. This was an excellent spot to exercise my envy: not only did the growers sport 36 varieties, from snow white to electric blue, but there was an ocean view to boot. Fortunately, the mopheads are grown solely for the cut flower trade, and I only need to pay a hefty shipping fee to bring them the 3,000 miles home. • It seems my devotion to hydrangea as a cut flower must be tested. In the vase, hydrangeas are capricious. One minute they are perky pompoms and the next—as if knowing they have been snipped from their true habitat—they wilt. The blossoms can, in most cases, be revived by recutting the stems and submerging the flowers in a basin of cool water for a few hours. Constant watering is required to cope with their troublesome nature, but I will continue to love them, despite their faults, because they share the vase so well with a huge variety of flowers.

Amethyst glass vases impart deep purple tints to the violet
hydrangeas, maroon dahlias 'Ryan,' mauve Australian
scaevola and blue nepeta 'Six Hills Giant.'

breeders of *Hydrangea macrophylla* have been tempting me with a wide array of hybrid mopheads from the palest pastels to deepest cobalt blue. The blossoms of the double rose hydrangeas tipped with white are so large, they could be mistaken for a fancy double pelargonium. In fact, hydrangeas are so fickle about color it is difficult to identify one variety from another since their shade is dependent on soil acidity. With this in mind, the hydrangeas for the bouquet recipes below should be motivated by color rather than named variety. The bouquet (*below left*) was made from ten heads of purple hydrangea and ten large garden dahlias. Lavender, scacvola, and salvia were added for lightness and air.

GREEN WITH ENVY

Chartreuse zinnia 'Envy,' immature sedum 'Autumn Joy,' and rose hydrangea tipped in white are supported by a floral frog inside the pedestaled painted English porcelain vase.

DELFT BLUES AND WHITES

Dahlia 'L'Ancresse,' deep blue-purple hydrangeas (such as 'Nikko Blue'), white hydrangeas (such as 'Madame Emile Mouillere') and pale blue-white bicolor hydrangeas occupy a cylindrical blue-and-white Delft vase.

ODE TO THE HYDRANGEA
By Peter Richmond ★

Hydrangeas are of two minds
When it comes to coloration,
Depending on the soil's tastes
And national location.

West Coast beds where alkaline
Doth sweeten all the soil,
Will tend to bloom with pinkish tinge:
A rose shade for your toil.

But dirt that's high in acids,
As our East Coast beds will be,
Will want to give you flowers
Blooming blue for all to see,

But should you wish to alter
Nature's natural progression
Give a mind to our advice
And heed a little lesson:

In Western plots, for blue to grow,
Add peat moss to your beds
(Aluminum sulphate also works,
But the rhyming hurts our heads)

In Eastern reaches if you find
Your heart's still set on pink,
Then just add lime to sweeten things:
The color will be fine (we think).

★*Peter Richmond, a magazine writer, is married to Melissa Davis.*

personal notes: ⸻⸻⸻⸻

⸻⸻⸻⸻⸻⸻⸻⸻

⸻⸻⸻⸻⸻⸻⸻⸻

⸻⸻⸻⸻⸻⸻⸻⸻

⸻⸻⸻⸻⸻⸻⸻⸻

WHAT COULD BE MORE INNOCENT THAN

A TABLE THEME OF WHITE ON WHITE?

POTAGER

The potager is one of the newest incarnations at Weatherstone. The project was spurred partly by inspiration and partly by necessity. I had attended a dinner celebrating the restoration of Louis XIV's enclosed vegetable and cutting garden at Versailles and was taken with the order and efficiency of the plan. I was in need of a fenced garden myself in Connecticut since the deer decimated anything that photosynthesized. My space, however, was limited to human, not kingly proportions. Over the winter, using the Sun King's design as a catalyst, I sketched out a plan for the potager. In early spring, the rustic wooden fences girded with wire were built and painted a weathered grey for a touch of New England charm. As the soil began to thaw, my plans drawn during the cold nights of winter became reality. After clearing a crop of spring bulbs, we planted the food and flowers that would see us through the summer. Our aim was to take as much advantage of vertical space as possible for its architectural element, while retaining the horizontal geometry of the defined squares. As you can see, we squeezed in a bountiful harvest for table and vase.

When I designed the potager, I had to deal with established reality: The main path through the garden was immutable, and the entire dimension of the garden was restricted by twenty-foot viburnum hedges. Oddly, the main path through the "room" bisected the sides unevenly, making the left enclosure narrower than the right. Since the right side was wider, it could accommodate my more formal plan. In the spring, we divided the right side of the potager into four 16-foot squares, each defined by Belgian blocks laid flush with the soil. Knowing that this would be a high-maintenance garden, we planted all our vegetable and flower seedlings closer together than recommended, hoping to cut down on weeding but offering an open invitation to slugs. Overall, the plan proved a success, supplying a wave of flowers and vegetables for the house through spring, summer, and fall.

THE RIGHT SIDE

POTAGER MAINTENANCE LIST

- Pinch off lower yellow leaves from parsley
- Deadhead zinnia and marigold every other day
- Watch for mildew on zinnias and spray with fungicide
- Stake tall marigolds as needed
- Hill up potatoes as they grow
- Refresh path with mulch
- Check pots daily for water
- Thin carrots

- Replace harvested lettuces with young plants
- Sweep debris from Belgian block
- Inspect potatoes daily for Colorado potato beetle and pick off
- Run irrigation twice a week
- Tie vining tomatoes with biodegradable twine
- Mound leeks to blanch
- Watch for striped cucumber beetles; pick off early in morning

After the spring plantings were yanked, we dug in the summer seedlings awaiting in the hoophouses. 'Blue Solaise' leeks and 'Ruby' chard flanked the gated entrance. Guy Wolfe pots stood in the center of each square and were plànted with Florence fennel, 'Charlotte' Swiss chard, and hot pink *Petunia integrifolia*. We pulled the tulip bulbs that stood in the square and planted 'Toreador' marigolds and a mix of zinnias. The spring lettuces were planted in tidy triangles were replaced with more heat-tolerant varieties. The tall peas growing up the trellis were replaced with runner beans, and 'Starshine' corn was given space on each side of the bean and pea poles.

AND THE
LEFT SIDE

The narrow left side of the potager could not accomodate the proper geometry of King Louis' inspiration, so it was defined by less rigid rules. The space inside the fence was cut into four 14-foot squares stacked vertically. To achieve a less formal look (and to free up more space), we did not define the squares with Belgian blocks, but made shredded bark mulch paths 2½ feet wide, large enough to accommodate a wheelbarrow. We built five 2-foot paths between squares to have access to the vegetables and flowers. Hollyhocks 'Chatter's Double,' 'Nigra,' and 'Peaches and Dreams' stood guard on the left side of the fence, while sweet peas 'Maggie May,' 'Rosemary Verey' and 'Summer Breeze' flanked the right, clinging to the wire mesh lining the wood fence. Each square was edged in the spring with low-growing vegetables. In late June, the radishes and spinach were pulled and replaced with three varieties of onions: 'Ailsa Craig,' 'Rossa di Milano,' and 'Giallo di Milano.' The mâche edging gave way to 'Genovese' (best for pesto) and 'Purple Ruffles' basil, which looked striking bouncing off *Sanvitalia* 'Mandarin Orange,' a creeping zinnia. Chocolate cosmos and *Scabiosa* 'Ace of Spades' made an impressive statement in the center squares. Teepees of scarlet runner beans punctuate the first and last square, while cardoon occupied the corners of the front and back bed. Low trellises were planted with 'Jack Be Little' pumpkins and 'Amira' cucumbers but were victims of squash beetle infestations that sapped them of vigor. The rear squares were reserved for eggplant 'Little Fingers' and 'Rosa Bianca,' 'Presto,' 'Touchon,' and 'Bolero' carrots, 'Sessantina Grossa' broccoli raab, and assorted hot and sweet peppers.

The growing space, though large by suburban standards, was not excessive, so I had to grow up, then decided I loved the architectural feel of it. The vertical elements included a dovecote, bean teepees, trellises, and hollyhocks. The hollyhocks were a favorite entree of the dreaded Japanese beetle. You will hear more about that later. . . .

enjoy

After months of planning and working, when the garden has finally yielded to my vision, the final reward is the simple pleasure of Seeing It Be. Although the process was stimulating and the conquered challenges gave me a sense of accomplishment, I have reached an age when I need to sit down and take in the fruits of all the labor. Savoring the smell of basil, tasting the citric ting of perfectly ripe tomatoes, and toasting the garden with a good glass of wine may be as close to tranquillity as I shall ever come. I encourage you to do the same. So kick back, stop and smell the roses—or in this case, basil—and enjoy what you and Mother Nature have created.

WE INVITE YOU TO SIT DOWN AND
TAKE IN THE FRUITS OF ALL YOUR LABORS

The following vegetables were planted in the Weatherstone potager. We did have some crop failures such as 'Painted Serpent' and 'Suyo Long' cucumber, but that could have been due to an overly wet spring and cucumber beetles.

ARUGULA

BASIL:
'Sweet Genovese'
'Purple Ruffles'

BEANS, BUSH:
'Goldkist' wax bean
'Roma II'

BEANS, FRENCH FILET:
'Tavera' French filet

BEANS, POLE:
'Cranberry'
'Emerite'
'Kentucky Blue'
'King of the Garden'

BEETS:
'Pronto'
'Golden'

BROCCOLI RAAB:
'Sessantina Grossa'
'Cima di Rapa'

BRUSSELS SPROUTS:
'Valiant'

CARDOON:
'Gigante'

CARROTS:
'Presto'
'Touchon'
'Bolero'

CELERIAC:
'Diamant'
'Mentor'

CHARD:
'Charlotte'

CORN:
'Starshine'
'Black Aztec'

CUCUMBER:
'Suyo Long'
'Amira'
'Painted Serpent'

EGGPLANT:
'Garden Mix'
'Little Fingers'
'Rosa Bianca'

GREENS:
'Tatsoi'
'Mizuna'

LEEK:
'Blue Solaise'

LETTUCE:
'Bronze Arrow'
'Four Seasons'
'Rough d'Hiver'
'Little Gem'
'Black Seeded Simpson'
'Mighty Red Oak'
'Buttercrunch'
'Green Ice'

MACHE:
'Coquille'
'Elan'

MELON:
'Charentais Charmel'

MESCLUN:
'Tangy Mix'

MUSTARD:
'Green Wave'

ONION, BULB:
'Ailsa Craig Exhibition'
'Giallo di Milano'
'Rossa di Milano'

ONION, BUNCHING:
'Deep Purple'
'Evergreen Hardy White'

POTATO:
'Yukon Gold'
'Russian Banana'
'Red Pontiac'

PEA:
'Carouby de Maussane'
'Sugar Snap'

PEPPERS, HOT:
'Anaheim'
'Hot Mix'

PEPPERS, SWEET:
'Corno di Toro'
'Nardello'
'Sweet Mix'

PUMPKIN:
'Jack Be Little'
'Small Sugar'

RADISH:
'Red Beret'
'Protection Racket'

SPINACH:
'Tyee'

SQUASH, SUMMER (crop failure):
'Milano' zucchini
'Sunburst' pattypan

SQUASH, WINTER (crop failure):
'Delacata'

TOMATILLO:
'Toma Verde'

TOMATO:
'Early Girl'
'San Marzano Paste'
'Sungold'
'Super Sweet 100' cherry
'Sweet Tangerine'
'Yellow Pear'

GARDEN JOURNAL

DATE:

GARDEN LOCATION:

PLANTS:

COMMENTS / RESULTS:

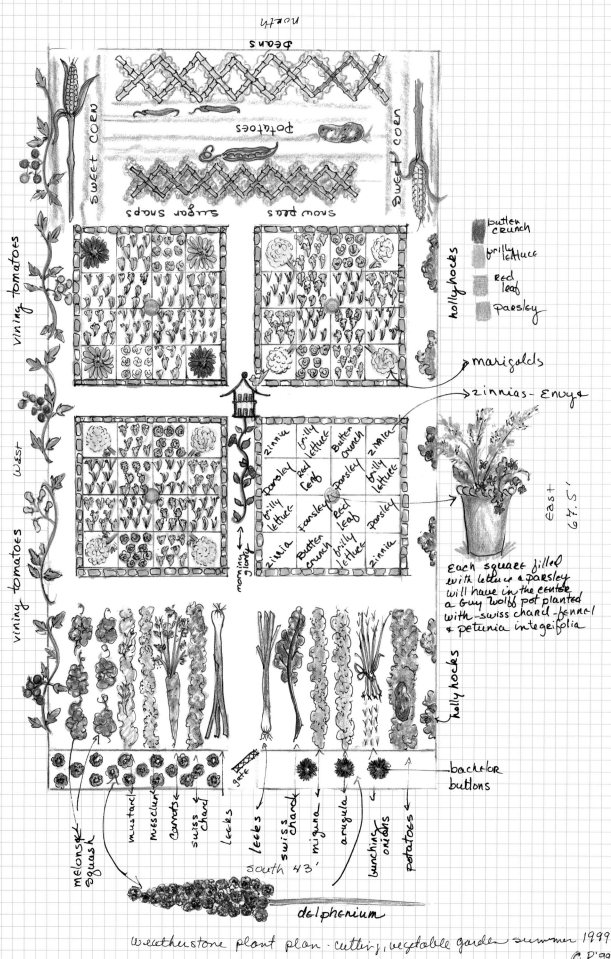

north

beans

Potatoes

SWEET CORN   Sweet corn

sugar snaps   snow peas

vining tomatoes

West

vining tomatoes

butter crunch
frilly lettuce
red leaf
parsley

hollyhocks

marigolds

zinnias - Envy≠

zinnia / frilly lettuce / Butter crunch / zinnia
parsley / red leaf / parsley / frilly lettuce
frilly lettuce / parsley / red leaf / parsley
zinnia / Butter crunch / frilly lettuce / zinnia

morning glory

east
67.5'

Each square filled
with lettuce & parsley
will have in the centre
a Guy Wolff pot planted
with swiss chard - fennel
& petunia integrifolia

hollyhocks

bachelor buttons

melons ≠ squash
mustard
mesclun
carrots
swiss chard
leeks

leeks
swiss chard
mizuna
arugula
bunching onions
potatoes

gate

south 43'

delphenium

Weatherstone plant plan · cutting, vegetable garden summer 1999

C.R.'99

ADDITIONAL NOTES / INSPIRATIONS / REMEMBER NEXT YEAR

END PAPERS

THE JAPANESE BEETLE

Every summer, usually by the second week of July, I am the host of the eighth deadly plague: The Japanese Beetle. These ungrateful visitors come in swarming hoards to gnaw and rip their way through my innocent roses, leaving them in tattered shreds. The garden staff at Weatherstone is armed for the invasion with cans of soapy water, but most of the damage is done at night. There is no sleep for the wicked Popillia japonica.

I once read the drollest of understatements: "Adult Japanese beetles are gregarious by nature." Right. More like sex-starved freshman frat boys. I prefer to think of them as the spawn of an evil nuclear survivalist cult. They are impervious to pesticides, unaffected by extreme weather conditions, and anathema to potential predators. Even if birds could penetrate their lacquered scarab shells, Japanese beetles apparently taste awful and are passed over for more succulent prey. My guess is that these beetles are fond of each other's company because no one else will have anything to do with the vile creatures.

Of course Japanese beetles don't just limit themselves to my roses. They are also despoilers of hollyhocks, grapevines and more than 250 other species of flowering plants and shrubs. When in the larval stage, the pre-beetles have voracious appetites. They feed on grassroots leaving huge brown clumps of matted dead turf. In a fitting bit of gardening irony, moles are the grubs' sole predators. Treatments of Milky Spore, a harmless microscopic bacteria, are reportedly successful at keeping the grubs at bay for decades. This is a fine solution for someone with an acre or less, but not particularly practical if your "lawn" is 60 acres.

As you can see, my war with the Japanese beetle has been a difficult battle fought with a puny arsenal. But last summer I reached a new plateau. I was able to take a beetle in coitus interruptus *and flatten it between my bare thumb and forefinger. Perhaps my moxie will not save the buds, but my revenge was sweeter than the roses' scent.*

CONTRIBUTORS

With her unerring eye, Sylvie Becquet has commuted from Paris for the past three years to chronicle the seasons, first in A Passion for Flowers *and now for* the Notebook. *Despite endless hours photographing the frenzied events from Connecticut to New York to Paris, from garden to kitchen, she has remained my good friend.*

When not knee-deep in well-composted manure, Melissa Davis, a veteran of The Washington Post *and* The Miami Herald, *brings her zeal for horticulture, food, writing, and editing to Weatherstone's table. She translates my actions and deeds into words.*

As the only male facilitator in the Weatherstone camp, Placido de Carvalho lends his ceaseless equanimity to the ongoing operation that is Weatherstone. Placido is the majordomo who makes it all happen and is the master of can-do optimism.

Margarida de Carvalho brings the excitement and exotica of Portuguese cuisine to rural Connecticut. Her spirit of cooperation matches that of her husband. Informal polls show that her vinaigrette is unequaled anywhere. We have tried torture, but she will not reveal the recipe.

Growing up in the kitchen of her father's New York City restaurant, Nancy Quattrini has known her way around a bèchamel since birth. Her zest for experimentation and her adventurous palate have kept us more than (ten pounds is a good guess) satisfied.

Nora Holmes came on board after the revered Terry Edwards retired. Terry's protègè has blossomed into a talented and hardworking head gardener. Kudos to Nora for trying to police my plant greed. She accepts defeat and brilliantly finds space for my new acquisitions.

Molly McCarthy holds down the fort in New York City. Functioning as my right and left hand, she keeps us all organized. Despite strenuous efforts and enticements, Molly declines condiments and meat.

Susan Poglitsch came to Weatherstone after more than a decade of experience in the floral trade. In the process of working on books and other media projects, I found in Susan a creative and talented striver who saves my life in the flower department.

I would also like to thank Rosa, Eddie and Delores. Special thanks also to Joanne, Tom, Carol, Nino, Randy and Joel. Thanks Mittie Ann for the hand-holding.

The Dogs:
At 17 human years, Pookie Roehm rules the roost as head dog and leading asparagus connoisseur. My beloved West Highland terrier is as much a part of Weatherstone as I am. Stoneleigh, strutting her Scottie stuff, has bohemian tastes. Her favorite sport is fishing for frogs, and she can dig a hole faster than I can. The German Shepherd Ike is the proverbial bull in the china shop. But like his mates, he is an avid gardener. Ike can often be spotted in his role as The Great Protector sleeping on top of newly planted perennials. Annie, the baby, makes us all laugh as she rips through every garden burying bones. Stoneleigh has taken her on as a work in progress and never leaves her side.

THE SOURCE GUIDE

ROSES:
The following companies offer a wide selection of mail order roses grown on their own rootstock:

Petaluma Rose Company
P.O. Box 750953
Petaluma, CA 94975
Tel: 707-769-8862
Fax: 707-769-0394
www.sonic.net/~petrose

Pickering Nurseries, Inc.
670 Kingston Rd.
Pickering, Ontario
Canada L1V 1A6
Tel: 905-839-2111
Fax: 905-839-4007

Roses of Yesterday & Today
Arena Rose Co.
803 Browns Valley Rd.
Watsonville, CA 95076
Tel: 831-724-3537

Vintage Gardens Antique Roses
2833 Old Gravenstein Hwy. South
Sebastopol, CA 95472
Tel: 707-829-2035
Fax: 707-829-9516
www.vintagegardens.com

General rose information:
http://www.rose.org

A site devoted to roses and gardeners who cultivate them:
http://www.rosarian.com

The American Rose Society:
http://www.ars.org

Yesterday's Rose offers information on old-fashioned roses:
http://www.Country-Lane.com/yr

Frequently asked questions about roses:
http://www.mc.edu/~nettles/rofaq/rofaq-top.html

HOT FLOWERS:
The following companies have a good selection of seed packets in individual colors, especially zinnias, cosmos, marigolds and sunflowers:

Johnny's Selected Seeds
310 Foss Hill Rd.
Albion, ME 04910
Tel: 207-437-9294
Fax: 800--437-4290
www.johnnyseeds.com

Park Seed
One Parkton Ave.
Greenwood, SC 29647
Tel: 800-845-3369
Fax: 800-275-9941
www.parkseed.com

Seymour's Selected Seeds
P.O. Box 1346
Sussex, VA 23884
Tel: 803-663-3084
Fax: 888-739-6687

Stokes Seed Co.
P.O. Box 548
Buffalo NY 14240
Tel: 716-695-6980
Fax: 888-834-3334

Thompson & Morgan
P.O. Box 1308
Jackson, NJ 08525
Tel: 800-274-7333
Fax: 888-466-4769

How to order annual seeds from Great Britain:
http://annualflowers.com/discovering/ordering.html

HYDRANGEAS:
American Hydrangea Society
P.O. Box 11645
Atlanta, GA 30355
Membership is $15 yearly which also entitles individual to The American Hydrangea Society Newsletter published quarterly.

The following nurseries specialize in mail-order hydrangea plants:
Bell Family Nursery
6543 South Zimmerman Rd.
Aurora, OR 97002
Tel: 503-651-2887

Carroll Gardens
444 East Main St.
Westminister, MD 21157
Tel: 410-848-5422
Fax: 410-867-44112

Louisiana Nursery
5853 Highway 182
Opelousas, LA 70570
Tel: 318-948-3696
Fax: 318-942-6404

Wilkerson Mill Gardens
9595 Wilkerson Mill Rd.
Palmetto, GA 30268
Tel: 770-463-2400
Fax: 770-463-9717

PERENNIALS:
Cooley's Gardens
P.O. Box 126
Silverton, Oregon 97381
Tel: 503-873-5463
Fax: 503-873-5812
Large selection of tall bearded irises.

Milaeger's Gardens
4838 Douglas Ave.
Racine, WI 53402
Tel: 414-639-2371
Fax: 414-639-1855
Orders: 800-669-9956
www.milaegers.com

Schreiner's
3629 Quinaby Rd.
Salem, OR 97303
Orders: 800-525-2367
Tel: 503-393-3232
Specializing in bearded iris.

Excellent web site for information on perennials and references to other perennial web sites:
http://www.uvm.edu/~pass/perry

TOMATOES:
Tomato Growers Supply Co.
P.O. Box 2237
Fort Meyers, FL 33902
Tel: 888-478-7333
Fax: 888-768-3476
www.tomatogrowers.com
Huge variety of seeds and grower supplies.

Totally Tomatoes
P.O. Box 1626
Augusta, GA 30903
Tel: 803-663-0016
Fax: 888-477-7333
Seeds for the home grower.

CORN:
Stokes Seed Co.
(See Hot Flowers)
Good selection of hybrid corn seed.

R.H. Shumway Seedsman
P.O. Box 1
Route1 Whaley Pond Rd.
Graniteville, SC 29829
Tel: 803-663-9771
Fax: 888-437-2733
Recommended for open-pollinated seeds.

PEACHES:
Adams Country Nursery, Inc.
P.O. Box 108
26 Nursery Lane
Aspers, PA 17304
Tel: 717-677-8105
Fax: 677-4124
www.acnursery.com
More than 65 varieties of peach trees available.

GARDEN FURNITURE AND ACCESSORIES:
Bluestone Main
120 Petaluma Blvd. North
Petaluma, CA 94952
Tel: 707-765-2024

Treillage, Ltd.
418 E 75th St
New York, NY 10021
Tel: 212-535-2288
Fax: 212-517-6589
Specializing in garden ornaments.

Despalles
76 Boulevard St Germain
Paris 75005
Tel: 01 43 54 28 98
Fax: 01 43 29 74 87

Le Cédre Rouge
Magasin Ch,telet
22 Avenue Victoria
Paris 75001
Tel: 01 42 33 71 05

CAKES:
Collette Peters
Colette's Cakes
681 Washington St
New York, NY 1001
Tel: 212-366-6530

Sylvia Weinstock Cakes Ltd.
273 Church Street, 3rd Floor
New York, New York 10013
Tel: 212-925-6698

PAPERS AND RIBBONS:
Mokuba
18 Rue Montmartre
Paris 75001
Tel: 01 40 13 81 41
Fax: 01 45 08 16 91

Papier Plus
9 Rue Pont Louis Philippe
Paris 75004
Tel: 01 42 77 70 49
Fax: 01 48 87 37 60

Hyman Hendler & Sons
67 W 38th St
New York, NY 10018
Tel: 212-840-8393
Fax: 212-704-4237

M & J Trimmings
1008 Avenue of the Americas
New York, NY 10018
Tel: 212-391-6200
Fax: 212-764-5854

Kate's Paperie
561 Broadway
New York, NY 10012
Tel: 212-941-9816
8 W 13th St
New York, NY 10011
Tel: 212-633-0570
1288 3rd Ave
New York, NY 10021
Tel: 212-396-3670

LINENS AND CHINA:
Bed Bath & Beyond
620 Avenue of the Americas
New York, NY 10011
Tel: 212-255-3550
Fax: 212-229-1040

Crate & Barrel
Various locations
Tel: 800-323-5461

Frette Inc.
799 Madison Ave.
New York, NY 10021
Tel: 212-988-5221
Fax: 212-988-5257

James Robinson Inc.
480 Park Ave.
New York, NY 10022
Tel: 212-752-6166
Fax: 212-754-0961
A wide selection of antique china.

Schweitzer Linens
1132 Madison Ave.
New York, NY 10028
Tel: 212-249-8361
Fax: 212-737-6328